Designing and Developing Library Intranets

For the past decade, e-mail has been the preferred method of internal communication in libraries. However, relying on email for organizational knowledge management seems a bit like storing birth certificates, car titles, and deeds in a pile of junk mail: the important documents are lost amongst other items of only minimal or fleeting importance. A successful intranet can provide a secure place for information exchange and storage; however, in order to be successful, a library intranet must be easy to use, have the functionality desired by its users, and be integrated into the daily workflows of all library staff. Accomplishing this can be challenging for web librarians.

The book covers, among other topics, third-party hosting; the use of freely available blog and wiki software for internal staff communication; and developing library intranets in ColdFusion, Microsoft SharePoint, and the open source Drupal content management system (CMS). More importantly, the authors examine in detail the human factors, which, when not thoroughly addressed, are more often the cause for a failed intranet than the technology platform.

This book was published as a special issue of the *Journal of Web Librarianship*.

Nina McHale is Assistant Systems Administrator at the Arapahoe Library District, USA.

Designing and Developing Library Intranets

Edited by
Nina McHale

Routledge
Taylor & Francis Group

LONDON AND NEW YORK

First published 2013
by Routledge
2 Park Square, Milton Park, Abingdon, Oxon, OX14 4RN

Simultaneously published in the USA and Canada
by Routledge
711 Third Avenue, New York, NY 10017

Routledge is an imprint of the Taylor & Francis Group, an informa business

British Library Cataloguing in Publication Data
A catalogue record for this book is available from the British Library

ISBN13: 978-0-415-62356-8

Typeset in Garamond
by Taylor & Francis Books

Publisher's Note
The publisher would like to make readers aware that the chapters in this book may be referred to as articles as they are identical to the articles published in the special issue. The publisher accepts responsibility for any inconsistencies that may have arisen in the course of preparing this volume for print.

Contents

CONTENTS

Introduction

For more than a decade, e-mail has been the preferred method of internal communication and information sharing in many libraries. However, relying on e-mail for organizational knowledge management seems a bit like keeping your birth certificate, car title, and deed to your home mixed in a pile with grocery store fliers and bills: the important pieces of information are mixed with items of only fleeting or minimal importance. The solution to organizing library policies, procedures, meeting minutes, and other documents that ultimately preserve an organization's history seems easy—all it takes is an intranet. Developing library intranets, on the other hand, has left many Web librarians scratching their heads and wondering, "I built it; why didn't they come?" Why are intranets such a challenge, even for information professionals?

Intranet users are perplexed by the lack of adoption and use among their colleagues as well. In a recent intranet training session at Auraria Library, I paused to ask my colleagues if they had any questions. One of them raised her hand and asked, "How do we make people use it?" My answer was that while we cannot enforce participation, our goal ought to be to make the intranet—in our case, a local installation of MediaWiki—so easy and fun to use that it became a natural part of everyone's workflow. To accomplish this, an intranet must be easy to use, have functionality desired by its users, and be thoroughly integrated into the everyday work environment. I freely admit that I approached *Journal of Web Librarianship* editor Jody Condit Fagan with the idea for this special issue so I could explore how others, who were also charged with developing a library intranet as I was, were successful.

Web 2.0 has opened up possibilities not only for the ways in which we communicate and provide services externally to our patrons but also the ways in which we collaborate and share organizational information internally. What were once unidirectional channels of information broadcast down from administration are now collaborative spaces used extensively in strategic planning processes. Does the addition of Web 2.0 features, functionality, and tools help librarians unlock the intranet riddle? Read this issue to find out!

First and foremost, an intranet needs a home. Ideally, this home would be space on a local server; however, this type of environment is not always possible, nor is what is available necessarily one's first choice. This special issue of *JWL* begins with an article by David Hodgins, access services librarian at the Kraemer Family Library, University of Colorado at Colorado

Springs. The campus IT department at UCCS would not allow library staff to install Web 2.0 tools, so Hodgins and his colleagues implemented MediaWiki and WordPress on commercial server space. Hodgins shares how this was accomplished and offers some of the lessons learned. University of Massachusetts Medical School Librarians Robert Vander Hart, Barbara Ingrassia, Kerry Mayotte, Lisa A. Palmer, and Julia Powell describe an almost opposite scenario, one in which the campus Web development environment—ColdFusion—was not a first choice but one that the authors made work. As a result, the Lamar Soutter Library's 2.0 intranet includes a wiki, blog, a discussion forum, and a photo collection manager.

The next group of articles focuses on librarians who chose blogs and wikis for intranet and/or internal communication environments. Kristen Costello, systems librarian, and Darcy Del Bosque, emerging technologies librarian, both at the University of Nevada, Las Vegas University Libraries, find that while a wiki increased staff satisfaction with internal communication, the use of blogs did not. Next, Becky Yoose, bibliographic systems librarian at Miami University, provides a case study of wiki use at King Library. In addition to describing the transition from using MediaWiki to using PBWorks wikis, she discusses the state of Web 2.0 "best practices" and finds them lacking. Keven Jeffery, digital technologies librarian at San Diego State University, and Ellie Dworak, reference services coordinator at Boise State University, relate how they marketed and supported their intranet wiki at San Diego State University after implementation. They also offer valuable advice aimed at preventing common mistakes that can lead to intranet failure.

Because Microsoft SharePoint is a popular out-of-the-box Web management tool, it should come as no surprise that many libraries turn to it when seeking to implement an intranet quickly on limited in-house resources. Bohyun Kim, digital access librarian at the Medical Library of Florida International University, describes her experiences implementing SharePoint in a brand new library with a staff of five. Even on a scale this small and without an organizational history, Kim notes Web 2.0 features did not automatically make a collaborative intranet environment easier to achieve. Emerging technologies librarian David Dahl describes how SharePoint was used by the Reference Department at Towson University's Albert Cook Library. Personal touches in the marketing and support of the department portal, such as incentivizing intranet use with a quarterly award given to library staff, were instrumental in making their intranet a success. The experiences of the document management team at the University of Maryland University College round out this trio of SharePoint articles with a description of how the department greatly improved efficiency with a similar departmental portal approach. Jennifer Diffin, Fanuel Chirombo, Dennis Nangle, and Mark de Jong's migration from shared network drives and three-ring binders filled with paper copies of procedures illustrates just how effective a successful intranet can be, with the end result being improved services to students and faculty.

The last three articles focus on developing intranets in-house from the ground up using the open-source content management system Drupal. With a focus on project management, Paul Sharpe, head of Liaison Services, and Rachel Vacek, head of Web Services, describe the transition from static Web pages into Drupal at the University of Houston Libraries. A testament to their success was the decision to eliminate internal e-mail mailing lists. Next, Jason Battles, head of the Web Services Department at the University of Alabama Libraries, discusses the importance of making an intranet a truly collaborative space. Drupal gave him and his colleagues the flexibility to make the intranet truly a "one-stop shop" for internal information needs. Finally, Amanda Etches-Johnson, user experience librarian, and Catherine Baird, marketing, communications and outreach librarian, both from McMaster University, echo Battles' emphasis on collaboration, noting "the days of top-down communication are—or should be—behind us." As with Sharpe and Vacek, Etches-Johnson and Baird place emphasis on the project management process.

Apart from environments, platforms, 2.0 tools, and technical issues, the most important takeaway from these articles is not to underestimate the previously mentioned human factors. Intranets must be easy to use, they must have functionality desired by users, and they must be integrated into daily workflows. Even factors that seem small to the techie types developing the intranets (for me personally, it was expecting users to maintain separate user accounts and to learn wikitext) can post huge barriers to intranet users, which ultimately result in underuse—or worse, failure—of an intranet. Fortunately, many development tools discussed in this issue of *JWL* have solutions for LDAP-integrated authentication and WYSIWYG editing environments.

On a final note, I'd like to mention our foray into Editing 2.0: the authors and I used a PBWorks wiki to organize and submit proposals and documents to this issue of *JWL*. All the authors could view one another's proposals, which gave each of them a sense of what specific niche in the issue they could each fill. When it came time to submit final drafts and the accompanying cover letters and image files, the wiki helped us all keep track of which copy of an article was the authoritative one, something I confess that I always struggle with as an editor. When it came time to hand off the content to *JWL* editor Jody Condit Fagan, she simply visited the wiki and downloaded the final versions of all files, which were kept neatly in separate folders. Hopefully, the end result will be as enjoyable to read as it was to make.

Nina McHale
Editor

Dynamic Space for Rent: Using Commercial Web Hosting to Develop a Web 2.0 Intranet

DAVE HODGINS

Colorado State Library, Denver, Colorado, USA

The explosion of Web 2.0 into libraries has left many smaller academic libraries (and other libraries with limited computing resources or support) to work in the cloud using free Web applications. The use of commercial Web hosting is an innovative approach to the problem of inadequate local resources. While the idea of insourcing IT will seem daunting to some, the process of setting up and administering hosting and applications is remarkably accessible to staff with basic word processing and Web skills. This article demonstrates the degree to which recent advances in commercial Web hosting and open-source applications have reduced the process of administering Web services, once time consuming and technically demanding, to near point-and-click simplicity. This article reports on the Kraemer Family Library's use of commercial Web hosting to develop and host a Web 2.0 staff intranet. The staff of 9.5 full-time equivalent librarians and 21.5 full-time equivalent staff serve 8,000 students and 700 faculty and staff at the University of Colorado at Colorado Springs. The small number of library faculty and staff provided the opportunity to experiment with Web 2.0 concepts and applications. Since certain IT-supported requirements were lacking, the library looked for no- and low-cost ways to host the intranet outside the university computing environment. After researching the use of free Web applications, the library's planning team decided to build its intranet using open-source applications and commercial Web hosting.

When the Kraemer Family Library at the University of Colorado at Colorado Springs began planning a new staff intranet in 2008, the planning team looked to Web 2.0 for ways to facilitate and enhance communication and collaboration. The library had operated for several years without a formal intranet, relying on e-mail, word of mouth, and a shared network drive for many intranet functions. Its traditional Web services were conservative; Web 2.0 had not been explored or pursued. The planning team used a two-pronged strategy: reintroducing the usefulness of a staff intranet and acquainting library faculty and staff with new and emerging technologies.

Web 2.0 is more than a fashionable phrase; libraries have embraced it and spawned Library 2.0, a synthesis of Web 2.0 and traditional library services—sometimes reinventing those services. The principles that have made Web 2.0 so popular for public interfaces—lightweight and easy-to-use applications—apply equally to internal communication and collaboration. Web 2.0 breaks down barriers between high-level technology and average users' skills through the use of low-threshold interfaces that are understandable by users within a wide range of technological skills and experiences.

The library's planning team recognized the significance of Library 2.0 and desired to create a dynamic environment where staff could not only communicate, collaborate, and archive, but also play and learn. The team was also mindful that introducing a major change could deter staff buy-in (Fichter 2006). During planning, WordPress was the focus as the means to shift communication from e-mail to blogging and collaboration and MediaWiki to shift documentation from the shared network drive to a wiki format. While neither strategy was then employed at the library, most staff had some familiarity with blogs, and certainly everyone had experience with wikis from using Wikipedia (http://wikipedia.org).

WordPress and MediaWiki are popular open-source Web 2.0 applications. In addition to providing elastic platforms capable of supporting a few to several million users—Wikipedia, which uses the MediaWiki platform, has more than 11 million user accounts (Wikipedia contributors 2010)—they embody the very best in Web 2.0. Both applications promote open communication and collaboration, provide sophisticated front- and back-end functionality, include rich user and administrator interfaces, and are entirely free to use and modify. They are available as lightweight Web applications that are deployable in LAMP environments: Linux (server operating system), Apache (server software), MySQL (database software), and PHP (scripting language).

These plans were presented to the UCCS IT department. Although UCCS IT maintains a LAMP server, they denied the library's access to it. The IT department did, however, grant permission for the library's staff intranet to be maintained using off-campus computing resources. Its only stipulation was that no personally identifiable student information, such as student ID numbers and social security numbers, could be stored off campus. The team was disappointed but understood IT's position; at the time, Web 2.0 was an unfamiliar concept to UCCS IT, and it had concerns about its ability to support the software.

LITERATURE REVIEW

Web 2.0 solutions for intranets are increasing in popularity. Survey results from the 2006 Global Intranet Strategies Study found institutions looked favorably on blogs and wikis as tools for collaboration, and "40 percent of respondents have or plan to have internal blogs" (McConnell 2006, n.p.). A 2008 survey of university libraries across the globe revealed that, of 48 respondents, 33.3 percent actively used wikis for work, with 27.1 percent planning on using them (Chu 2009). A search of Information Science & Technology Abstracts produced numerous cases of libraries incorporating Web 2.0 technology into intranets. The planning team combed these and other resources to investigate ways that libraries overcame local IT limitations; the team found no mention of commercial Web hosting as a solution, though free Web applications and commercial software received numerous mentions.

Libraries and other groups have reported success using Web 2.0 intranet solutions in varying degrees of complexity, from small research groups to full content management systems (CMSs). In "Blogs and Wikis are Valuable Software Tools for Communication within Research Groups," the authors reported on the successful use of Typepad blogs for communication and recording lab records within research groups (Sauer, et al. 2005). Judith Kammerer (2009) reported on the use of SharePoint as a CMS for developing a Web 2.0 intranet in a hospital library. However, the team found no mention of using commercial Web hosting to implement Web 2.0, either for external or internal use.

The team, therefore, shifted its focus to the ways libraries were using free Web applications. The article "Putting Wikis to Work in Libraries" (Lombardo, Mower, and McFarland 2008) proved an excellent resource; the authors described, compared, and contrasted the use of free Web wikis with locally hosted solutions. The former were used by staff at the Eccles Health Sciences Library to collaborate on grant writing and a strategic plan, while the latter were used to develop a library policy manual. The authors concluded that free Web wikis "are very easy to use; not much building is required to link various documents and/or spreadsheets, and there is no need for local

IT support" and that locally hosted wikis "are much more robust" and do not suffer from the limitations in storage space and number of users that their free Web counterparts do (143).

There was evidence in the research of other libraries experimenting with free Web applications and then migrating to local solutions, as discussed by Sherab Chen in 2009 when she reported on the use of Google's free Blogger service to create a collaborative workspace for technical services staff. She noted that while the free Web blog was successful, they moved it to a local server when resources became available.

FROM PLANNING TO DEVELOPMENT

Free Web Apps

Web applications offer free (or inexpensive) solutions for harnessing Web 2.0 technology. Additionally, they are easy to use; for example, within minutes, users can register an account with Blogger, modestly customize the look of their blog, and publish content on the Web. With an e-mail address and basic word processing skills, users have an unimaginable wealth of freely available Web applications at their disposal. The team simply could not ignore the advantage that Web applications offered.

Initially, the focus was on blogging and group editing solutions; the Web services the team tested included Wordpress, Blogger, PBWorks, and Google Docs. The end result was a determination to use hosted, open-source applications. Although each application tested performed well and separately achieved the goals within its narrow range of focus, it was decided that a limit to third-party-managed applications negatively affected three key areas of the project: flexibility, customizability, and security.

Hosted applications are necessarily less flexible and customizable than their stand-alone counterparts; in order for companies to provide free services, such as blogs, photo galleries, and file managers, certain functionality is withheld from users. While the Web applications tested here provided inexpensive and powerful solutions, certain characteristics made them poor choices as intranet solutions. Chief among concerns were the inability to modify or enhance core functionality and limited access to data.

The beauty of open source applications lies in the ability to personalize them through aesthetic and functional changes and improvements. There is often a stark contrast between the potential of free Web applications and their hosted counterparts. WordPress.com and the separately available WordPress application serve as excellent examples that will be used throughout this article. WordPress.com offers free blogging accounts wherein users have modest control over the appearance of their site through the use of templates, widgets, and custom CSS. Core functionality, though, is immutable. The

WordPress application includes these same features but additionally allows the use of plug-ins and custom code to change not only the look but the functionality of one's site. Plug-ins, which can be installed and configured using the standard WordPress interface, allows users and administrators to modify or introduce functionality that would otherwise be impossible using a free WordPress account. Possible uses for plug-ins are quite numerous, including enabling enhanced security features, improved user management functions, and the integration of other Web 2.0 applications. A comprehensive database of free plug-ins is available at http://wordpress.org/extend/plugins/.

A key aspect of managing applications is the ability to retrieve or back up, en masse, user and application data and settings. Free Web applications use black-box methods for storing and retrieving data. The usual means for users to interact with their data is through the application's standard Web interface; data is not directly accessible using standard protocols like FTP or SSH. The methods available for wholesale download or backup vary greatly among applications. Some applications offer near-comprehensive means, while others are restrictive. PBWorks, for example, allows users to download a complete site backup that includes individual HTML files of each page and any uploaded files. WordPress, though, limits users to exporting their content (authors, pages, posts, categories, etc.) in single XML files. While this may be useful for migrating data to another blogging application, this lack of the ability to mass download uploaded files for backup purposes meant this application was unsuitable for the needs of this library.

The methods employed by both WordPress and PBWorks are decidedly less convenient than direct server access. The ideal setup would provide tools that simplify data retrieval while also allowing direct server access, maximizing the ability to migrate data to next-generation technologies. The team felt that using hosted applications, in addition to limiting the methods with which data could be retrieved, would bring exposure to the risk of losing data to the collapse or failure of the individual companies hosting its services.

The team also recognized and accepted that any data stored on remote servers could potentially be accessed by unauthorized individuals. It is the nature of the Web that standard security measures, such as usernames, passwords, sessions, etc., are deterrents rather than guarantees, which makes storing and retrieving data on the Web a calculated risk. With this in mind, each application's basic security functions were explored, especially as they related to user management and data preservation. Some applications offer some inherent protection through the use of data persistency and rich user management functions. WordPress manages users through roles, which carry with them varying levels of rights and permissions. In many of the applications researched, low-level users were able to create and edit content but not entirely delete it; that task that was reserved for editors and administrators.

Viability of Commercial Web Hosting

After carefully considering the suitability of free Web applications for use in an intranet, it was decided that the best way to maximize flexibility and customizability was by using open-source applications. WordPress and MediaWiki were selected as the foundation of the new intranet. Both are open-source applications, free to use and modify; however, they require access to PHP and MySQL, resources that were not available to the library. At a cost of $5 to $10 per month, commercial Web hosting promised to be an affordable way to acquire these and other resources necessary for the proposed Web 2.0 applications. The hosting package selected included access to a server running a LAMP setup, an adequate amount of data storage space and bandwidth, technical support, and a variety of tools that simplified the process of interacting with our server and services.

Some planning team members had previous experience using commercial Web hosting for personal Web sites and applications, so the team benefitted from some prior understanding of the process of working with remote resources and the skills necessary to be successful. The library is now in its third year of using commercial hosting for its intranet, and the team can confidently report the project was not technically demanding. The following skills were used: Internet browsing, word processing, file handling, and basic knowledge of HTML and CSS.

When confronted with issues beyond our immediate understanding, a variety of sources was consulted, including the host's customer service and Internet resources specific to Web 2.0 applications. A remarkable community has developed in support of WordPress and MediaWiki. Detailed online documentation is available for both products. WordPress hosts an active user forum, and MediaWiki offers a mailing list.

In addition to being usable by staff with average technology skills, implementing Web 2.0 using commercial hosting did not require any costly supplementary software. The hosting package here included a suite of tools for interacting with the server, but the following other freely available software was also employed:

- FileZilla: FTP client for accessing files on the server.
- Notepad: text editor for working with HTML and CSS files.
- Web browser: for accessing the intranet site, applications, and the server control panel.

The tools built into the selected applications were also used to advantage. WordPress and MediaWiki feature tools that simplify the processes of configuring the applications and managing users. WordPress, in particular, provides an excellent example of the best in Web 2.0; its control panel allows a variety of sophisticated functions, including file management and the ability to edit application files from within a browser.

Choosing a Host

The number of Web hosting companies is staggering, so much so that "services are so similar and interchangeable across vendors that they've been commoditized" (Guenther 2005, 59). When examining hosting packages, technical differences will be negligible. This means that for most, choosing the right host will depend on less measurable factors such as recommendations and reviews. The libraries' first foray into commercial hosting ended in disappointment when severe performance issues and extended server downtime was experienced. The host, recommended by word of mouth, suffered equipment failure that took several weeks to address. When reviewing hosting companies, it is wise to take note of the company's refund policy; a 30- to 90-day money-back guarantee should allow for sufficient time to fully evaluate the company's services. In this case, the service was canceled and a full refund received.

The second and current host, Host Gator (http://www.hostgator.com/), was also recommended by word of mouth. Additionally, online research results included many positive user reviews and a Better Business Bureau accreditation. As the team was wary of working with another unresponsive company, customer service was contacted via telephone, e-mail, and online chat to gauge the quality and efficiency of their customer service. The reward for this effort has been two years of dependable and nearly trouble-free service. One instance of degraded performance was experienced: the site slowed to a crawl because of heavy bandwidth use by another customer on our server. A call to customer service resolved the issue in a matter of minutes.

The Server

Companies are able to offer affordable hosting services through the use of shared hosting. Shared Web hosting is a model in which multiple customers share a single server. Most hosting packages allow customers to host multiple Web sites, so a single account might be located on a machine that serves ten or 100 Web sites. There is usually no way to know the exact specifications of the hardware being used. The only effective way to ensure that one's own services receive priority is to purchase dedicated hosting services, which can cost upward of $200 per month; reputable hosting companies usually list the specifications (such as processor speed and RAM allotment) for these servers.

Commercial Web hosts often make seemingly outrageous claims in regards to available bandwidth and disk space. It is not unusual to see both advertised as "unlimited." There is an important distinction in the way hosts and average users view disk space. Hosts provide unlimited disk space for content that is served via Web sites; many terms of services prohibit using disk space for static content. For example, while one can operate a photo gallery that serves tens of thousands of files, taking up several gigabytes of space, that same space could not be used to simply archive the content. Likewise, while the cumulative bandwidth one may use may not be strictly monitored, customers who use excessive bandwidth by streaming audio or video may find their services throttled or discontinued, as was the case with a customer with whom server space was shared.

Shared hosting presents two major concerns: performance and security. In terms of performance, the load on any given server will be affected by the number of Web sites it serves and the sites' respective traffic. The activities of one's server neighbors, such as serving bandwidth-intensive content like streaming audio and video, may adversely affect the performance of one's own site(s). Security is also a concern any time multiple users share a single device; given the right conditions, it is possible to use scripting languages and techniques to traverse directories and content on a server. To mitigate this, the user is responsible for ensuring that files and folders are assigned the appropriate permissions and that strict control is maintained over user names and passwords.

A shared hosting package costing $8 per month was the option here, and a domain name (uccslib.org) was purchased for an additional $8 per year. Customers who opt not to purchase a domain name must access their content via an IP address, often a cumbersome and clumsy task, especially if IP addresses are dynamically assigned and therefore subject to change on a regular basis.

The Server Software

Web hosting packages are normally offered with Linux servers, though the option to use Windows servers may be available. The hosting company of this library offers a choice, and the team opted for a Linux server, since the intended open source applications were built for a LAMP environment. The package also includes an extensive suite of applications that novice users will find useful, especially the control panel.

Host Gator offers the popular cPanel control panel, which is the central nervous system of our hosting services (see Figure 1). Accessible via the Web, cPanel is a collection of applications that reduces the processes of managing services and applications to near point-and-click simplicity. Several of the more useful applications are

- File manager: managing server files,
- FTP manager: accessing server files,
- MySQL manager: creating and modifying databases,

FIGURE 1 Screen capture of cPanel tools.

- PHPMyAdmin: accessing database files, and
- AWStats: managing Web statistics.

Accessing Files

The primary method for accessing server files is via FTP using FileZilla, which is available for free at http://filezilla-project.org/. After purchasing hosting services, an initial FTP username and password were provided. Additional FTP users can be created, and users' access can be limited by directory and file size. FTP clients are similar to file management software built into most operating systems. FTP is used to upload, download, delete, and modify permissions of files on the server.

cPanel includes a built-in file manager that offers the functions listed above and also allows for editing HTML files and extracting and compressing files (see Figure 2).

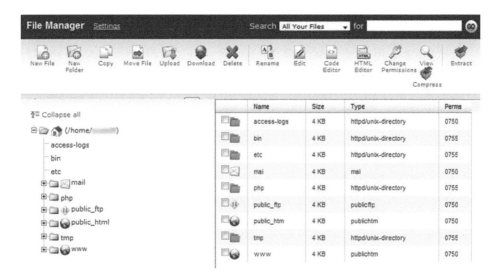

FIGURE 2 Screen capture of cPanel file manager.

Managing Databases

Database management can be a challenging aspect to any Web project. MySQL Databases, available in cPanel, automates the processes of creating, modifying, and deleting databases and database users (see Figure 3).

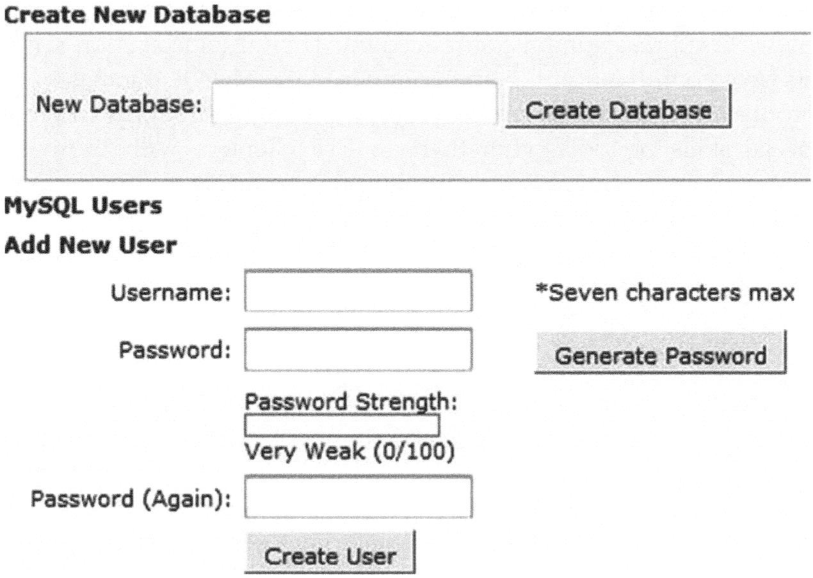

Create New Database

New Database: [ ] Create Database

MySQL Users

Add New User

Username: [ ] *Seven characters max

Password: [ ] Generate Password

Password Strength:
[ ]
Very Weak (0/100)

Password (Again): [ ]

Create User

FIGURE 3 Screen capture of cPanel database manager.

cPanel also comes equipped with PHPMyAdmin, an open-source software option for managing MySQL databases. PHPMyAdmin, which requires a basic understanding of relational databases, provides direct access to modify the structure of the databases and the raw data therein. While its inclusion in cPanel is a perk, it is not needed to install, configure, or administer applications like WordPress and MediaWiki.

Working with Applications

Our host offers an automated scripting program for installing and configuring selected applications. Fantastico, available in cPanel, can install a variety of applications, including WordPress, Drupal, Joomla, and TikiWiki. Fantastico automatically creates and configures any necessary databases; any required information is supplied, such as the installation directory, site name, and description, in the case of WordPress.

Manually installing applications requires additional steps but is equally technically unexacting. WordPress and MediaWiki feature Web installation scripts; after uploading the necessary files, users simply point their browser to the script to complete installation. This was the case when WordPress MU, a version of WordPress that enables multiple blogs and users to be managed using a single database and WordPress installation, was installed. To deploy WordPress MU, a database was first created along with a database user in cPanel, then it was uploaded the WordPress MU files to the server via FTP. Our browser was pointed to the installation script at http://www.uccslib.org/wordpressmu/wp-admin/install.php, supplied access information for the newly created database, and specified information for a new WordPress administrator account. Then the installation script created its own configuration file and configured the MySQL database.

From start to finish, the process took less than ten minutes and required no special skills or tools other than an FTP client, a Web browser, and the server's control panel. After installing the applications, their respective administrator interfaces was used to complete their setups, performing such functions as creating users, specifying privacy settings, and altering themes.

Backing up Data

Two methods to back up and, if necessary, restore data were used. The first method involves the backup function provided in cPanel, which allows for downloading the contents of the server file directory, downloading SQL backups of the databases, or both together as a complete site backup. The second method involves manually downloading files via FTP and individual SQL backups using PHPMyAdmin. Either method gives us a full backup of files and databases, both of which can be restored quickly and easily.

Staying Current

The most time-consuming aspect of maintaining these applications is keeping them current. Keeping software up to date is essential to security. Separate strategies are employed for updating WordPress and MediaWiki. WordPress includes an automatic software updater in its administrator interface that downloads, installs, and updates all necessary application files. Updating MediaWiki requires that these functions be performed manually. Updated files are downloaded from MediaWiki.com and then uploaded to the server via FTP.

CONCLUSION

Following a minor misstep with an unreliable host, hosting services have been reliable. With a minimal investment of staff time, open-source Web 2.0 applications were deployed, configured for internal use, and were modestly enhanced visually and functionally. Performing regular data and system backups, in tandem with regular software updates, has kept data safe and secure. Using popular open-source applications with large, community-driven support networks ensures the intranet will be sustainable and manageable by the next generation of staff.

In the future, the library hopes to further incorporate Web 2.0 functionality through a group calendar and file management software, and with some luck, the aging network drive may yet be retired. Planned improvements include a single login for multiple applications, either through the use of htaccess (server-level access) or custom scripting (modifying individual applications to use a single user database).

The library's decision to use commercial Web hosting as a way to develop a Web 2.0 intranet was a success. A modest investment of $100 per year has provided access to resources critical to implementing Web 2.0 concepts and technologies, resources that otherwise would have been unobtainable locally. For the library, this represented a shift from reliance on local resources to self-directed technology and innovation. The broader implication for academic libraries is that powerful technology resources are affordable, attainable, and usable by staff within a wide range of expertise and experience, even without local IT support.

REFERENCES

Chen, Sherab. 2009. Can blogging help cataloging?: Using a blog and other Web 2.0 tools to enhance cataloging section activities. *Library Resources & Technical Services* 53(4): 251–260.

Chu, Samuel Kai-Wah. 2009. Using wikis in academic libraries. *The Journal of Academic Librarianship* 35(2): 170–176.

Fichter, Darlene. 2006. Making your intranet live up to its potential. *Online* 30(1): 51–53.

Guenther, Kim. 2005. Understanding your Web hosting options. *Online* 29(3): 58–60.

Kammerer, Judith J. 2009. Migrating a hospital library Web site to SharePoint and expanding its usefulness. *Journal of Hospital Librarianship* 9(4): 408–418.

Lombardo, Nancy T., Allyson Mower, and Mary M. McFarland. 2008. Putting wikis to work in libraries. *Medical Reference Services Quarterly* 27(2): 129–145.

McConnell, Jane. 2006. Global intranet strategies survey results. *Globally Local Blog.* http://netjmc.typepad.com/globally_local/2006/10/global_intranet.html (accessed November 1, 2009).

Sauer, Igor M., Dominik Bialek, Ekaterina Efimova, Ruth Schwartlander, Gesine, Pless, and Peter Neuhaus. 2005. "Blogs" and "wikis" are valuable software tools for communication within research groups. *Artificial Organs* 29(1): 82–89.

Wikipedia contributors. Wikipedians. http://en.wikipedia.org/wiki/Wikipedia_users (accessed February 3, 2010).

Upgrading a ColdFusion-Based Academic Medical Library Staff Intranet

ROBERT VANDER HART, BARBARA INGRASSIA, KERRY MAYOTTE,
LISA A. PALMER, and JULIA POWELL

*Lamar Soutter Library, University of Massachusetts Medical School,
Worcester, Massachusetts, USA*

This article details the process of upgrading and expanding an existing academic medical library intranet to include a wiki, blog, discussion forum, and photo collection manager. The first version of the library's intranet from early 2002 was powered by ColdFusion software and existed primarily to allow staff members to author and store minutes of library team meetings. Other ColdFusion-based applications and functions were subsequently added, as were various other library documents and procedures. As a follow-up to the library's strategic plan, a library Staff Intranet Team was organized in early 2008 to reorganize the content of the intranet and to identify software tools that would allow greater staff participation in maintaining and updating intranet content. Early steps in the process included brainstorming, a card-sorting exercise, product research, a staff survey, and paper prototyping. The team focused on implementing various open-source, ColdFusion-based tools in order to accommodate existing technology, available budget, and time constraints. Challenges in implementing the tools included bypassing or modifying existing authentication systems and applying modifications that led to loss of native functionality. Despite usability testing and staff training, library staff have not universally welcomed or adopted all the new tools. Notwithstanding these challenges, the renovated staff intranet has shown promise in furthering the goals in the library's strategic plan to improve communication and facilitate collaboration among library staff.

Many organizations and institutions, whether for-profit, non-profit, or educational, use intranets to increase staff productivity. Intranets have evolved from unidirectional information channels between managers and employees to integrated workspaces that support collaboration, communication, daily operations, and information needs of staff (Martini, Corso, and Pellegrini 2009). Intranet tools like wikis, blogs, and discussion forums enable greater opportunities for staff collaboration. Possessing skills such as blogging, maintaining a wiki, and uploading and tagging photos may be vital for library staff in order to meet the evolving needs of both themselves and their patrons.

The University of Massachusetts Medical School, which opened in 1970, includes the graduate schools of medicine, nursing, and biomedical sciences. The Lamar Soutter Library, which is open to the public, is considered a medium-sized academic health sciences library. The library staff consists of almost 40 full-time equivalent employees and serves more than 1,100 students, 1,300 faculty, and thousands of additional researchers, clinicians, and employees.

Discussions about an intranet at the library began in 1999 and came to fruition in early 2002. At that time, the intranet was conceived of as a place for library teams and departments to author, edit, and retrieve meeting minutes and to archive reports. Several Web forms, developed by the library Web manager, facilitated the management of meeting minutes by library staff. Other new content, however, had to be added by the Web manager.

The intranet is hosted on a library-owned Web server running the Linux operating system. It is maintained by library staff members and powered by ColdFusion software from Adobe (http://www.adobe.com/products/coldfusion/). Library interest in ColdFusion stemmed from the university's decision in the late 1990s to use the software for its own Web site. Advantages of ColdFusion include easy application development, a low learning curve, and a simple tag-based language. The major disadvantage is the software cost (Langley 2007).

As a follow-up to the library's 2006 strategic plan (Lamar Soutter Library 2006), a cross-departmental intranet team was formed in early 2008. By this time, the library's intranet had outgrown its original conception and was hosting several locally developed ColdFusion-based applications necessary for some staff members to perform their duties. The Staff Intranet Team was charged to "identify content, a new organization, and potential tools (open source) to improve the functionality and ongoing maintenance (perhaps self-service) of the staff intranet" (Lamar Soutter Library 2008b, n.p.).

Overcome departmental barriers within the library that limit service to our patrons
- Share knowledge among library departments through integrated documentation in order to understand the best department to provide service.
- Establish a central repository of current and archived library-wide policies and procedures.

Improve intra- and cross-departmental communication so that all library departments can operate interdependently to improve the quality, quantity, and speed of information provided internally.
- Communicate to all staff new products and services at the library.
- Explore and implement opportunities to share expertise across departments such as short term assignments for a particular task or project.
- Provide new ways for staff to provide input on new and/or old services, policies, procedures and how they can be improved.

Foster an environment within the library conducive to collaboration.
- Explore ways library staff can actively participate in collaborative efforts.

FIGURE 1 Strategic plan goals and objectives related to the Staff Intranet Team's work.

The team thus had two main tasks: to reorganize the content of the intranet and to identify software tools that would allow greater staff participation in maintaining and updating intranet content. The team's charge addressed several goals and objectives in the library's strategic plan, which are listed in Figure 1.

Team members also hoped that as a result of their efforts, intranet use would increase and that incorporating collaborative tools would cultivate a greater community atmosphere in the library.

LITERATURE REVIEW

In their book *Intranets for Info Pros*, Mary Lee Kennedy and Jane Dysart made the following observation:

> There are an enormous number of technology choices to be made when looking at intranet applications, and custom-built applications continue to be a popular choice for many organizations. These choices can fluctuate depending on resident expertise, strength of senior sponsorship, technology integration costs, sophistication of user expectations, and (of course) available budget. (2007, 17)

Very little has been published in the library and information science literature about the use of ColdFusion as a technology choice for intranet applications. However, the published literature is rich with articles *about* intranets—their various uses and components and the process for developing them through the various and often interrelated phases of investigating, needs assessing, implementing, testing, promoting, training, adding and updating content, day-to-day oversight, and ongoing evaluation and revision.

Several articles were particularly helpful in informing the team's thinking as the project moved through its phases. Mel O'Brien and Jillian Wisbey (2008, 29) focused on what they called the "soft aspect" of the intranet: the "planning, implementation, management, evaluation … and integration … rather than the hard equipment and technological aspects." They offered helpful, specific suggestions for training, evaluation, promotion, and marketing and for dealing with issues and challenges. They emphasized the importance of four elements: people, process, content, and technology. In addition, Darlene Fichter (2005, 2006a, 2006b) and Darlene Fichter and Jeff Wisniewski (2008) offered specific ideas for designing effective intranets in the "Intranet Librarian" column in *Online*.

Joel Glogowski and Sarah Steiner (2008, 89) provided a brief general overview of wikis, noting they are "an ideal tool for online collaboration"; they also help facilitate interdepartmental communication and assure currency of content for policies, procedures, committee pages, schedules and sign-ups, price quotes for materials, etc. Georgia State University even includes "fun pages" for recipes and information on local restaurants. They have included a helpful "wiki posting guidelines and tag list" as an appendix in the article.

Lisa Cotter, Larnich Harije, and Suzanne Lewis (2006) addressed usability issues and applied principles of evidence-based librarianship to redevelop the Central Coast Health Service Library's intranet site. They provided specific suggestions for usability testing. The use of surveys is discussed in some detail by Sarah Robbins, Debra Engel, and James Bierman (2006).

PLANNING PROCESS

The library Staff Intranet Team met weekly from March through July 2008. Team membership consisted of representatives from all departments in the library and included professional and support staff. One of the team's first activities was a complete review of the contents of the intranet. As mentioned above, the intranet originally housed team and departmental minutes and reports, but by early 2008, its usage had greatly expanded to include the following ColdFusion-scripted applications: documentation for the library's strategic plan and disaster plan, training documents for the library's support staff career ladder program, a Web form to record service desk informational

TABLE 1 Seven Content Areas from Card Sorting Exercise

Content Area/Category	Specific Content Included
Statistics	Reports on: e-resource usage, catalog usage, gate count, service tracking log, month Web log analyzer
Staff Personal Profiles	Form to change password; form to update profile on the public Web site
Specific Supporting Applications	Circulation log "notebook"; service tracking log; e-journals list with ILL information; institutional repository name authority database
Library History/Archives	Library photographs and images; past staff meetings minutes and documents; past team minutes; past team reports
Current Awareness	Events and classes calendar; staff directory; current staff meeting minutes and documents; internal library newsletter; current team minutes
Staff-Generated Public Content	Web form for staff to author public Web site FAQ; Web site content request form for staff to initiate Web projects
Documentation	Staff meeting instructions; various PDF forms; library employee handbook; library disaster plan; intranet instruction manual; service tracking log; support staff career ladder program information; strategic planning documents; circulation log "notebook"; policies and procedures (including any on networked drives)

transactions, an application to manage author information in the library's institutional repository, a list of online journal subscriptions with accompanying title-level interlibrary loan information, and a library events calendar.

The team brainstormed additional content that was not on the intranet but could improve productivity if it were included. For example, many procedural documents were scattered on several networked drives and individual desktop computers and, therefore, were not as useful to the staff as they could be. Monthly usage reports for electronic journals, books, and the library Web site had also been developed. These Web pages were not linked to from the public Web site but also were not part of the intranet. In addition, many photographs had been taken at various library events and then stored on a networked drive. The team believed these images were a valuable part of the library's culture and history and discussed how they might be made more accessible and better organized.

The team recorded all the current and potential content of the intranet and performed an open card-sorting exercise. This exercise yielded seven broad content areas (see Table 1).

The card-sorting exercise and the preceding brainstorming and inventorying activities were done primarily to inform conceptual intranet reorganization efforts. The seven content areas, for example, would not necessarily coincide with specific sections of the intranet.

Next, a number of possible intranet software products were examined to identify the pros, cons, and features of each. Team members had identified several categories of products that could increase staff productivity, including wiki, blog, discussion forum, and photograph management applications. At this point, the team was faced with starting from scratch on the intranet, with the possibility of having to retool the existing applications into another scripting language. The other option considered was to keep the existing intranet applications and to find tools written for the current ColdFusion system. Because of the potential delay involved in rewriting existing applications, the team chose not to consider rescripting the existing applications into another language. For this reason, the content management system Drupal (http://drupal.org) and the wiki product MediaWiki (http://www.mediawiki.org) were not feasible options since they are written in the PHP scripting language. (See the "Implementation" section below for more details.)

It was important to assess the level and nature of staff usage of the intranet prior to any redesign efforts. Twenty-four library staff members (out of about 40) completed a June 2008 survey on their intranet usage. The survey's purpose was to get an idea of staff members' usage patterns on the intranet and to assess their comfort level with 2.0 tools. The first question asked how often the staff member logged into the intranet per week. Eleven respondents indicated one to two times per week, while ten stated they logged in at least five times per week. The survey also asked staff if they were using any Web-based tools such as wikis, blogs, instant messaging, Twitter, photo-sharing sites, document-sharing sites, social networking sites, tagging/bookmarking sites, or YouTube. Results indicated staff members were quite familiar with these tools, with the exception of Twitter.

The next major team activity was a paper prototyping exercise, an important step in the redesign and reorganization of the intranet's user interface. This simple element of "discount usability," popularized by Jakob Nielsen (2009), proved to be a relatively quick, easy, and helpful step in the redesign process. Members worked first individually and then in pairs with chart paper and markers and drew rough sketches of a reorganized intranet homepage. They critiqued the schematics and developed a Web model of a new homepage, complete with blog postings and a photo of the week. The mockup was shown to key library staff members and was further refined.

IMPLEMENTATION

The Staff Intranet Team submitted its final report on schedule in August 2008. Library management approved the report, including the proposed model for the reorganization of the intranet. The team was reconvened as the Staff Intranet Implementation Team in September 2008 and was charged with "transitioning the current Web site to a site that incorporates blogs, wikis, calendar applications, and photo sharing as needed, with the goal of maintaining security and limiting the need for multiple logins" (Lamar Soutter Library 2008a). Staff convenience necessitated the limitation of the number of logins. The team's charge specified that the new site should be in production by December 31, 2008.

The avoidance of multiple logins dictated that the team should focus its attention on solutions that would not direct staff members to remote Web sites. This, in turn, led the team to search for software, preferably freeware, that could be installed on the library's Web server. Since the existing intranet's system was ColdFusion-based, the team focused its search on applications written for that environment. It was also the system with which the library Web manager was most familiar.

Extensive testing of various software tools, which were discussed as part of the previous team's work, was a major component of the implementation team. The team selected four ColdFusion-based tools—Canvas ColdFusion Wiki, BlogCFC, Galleon ColdFusion Forums, and CFCPhotoBlog—from the RIAForge Web site (http://www.riaforge.org), a repository of open source projects built on Adobe technology. Both the wiki and the photo blog required the Model-Glue framework, which supports Web application development "by making the construction of object-oriented Web and rich internet applications a straightforward process" (Model-Glue Team 2009, n.p.).

Because these software packages are open source, in several instances the library Web manager was able to extend the tools' functionality to make them more useful to library staff. For example, he added tagging functionality to the photo collection software. This involved both modifying the ColdFusion templates and adding two fields to the MySQL data table. He also added TinyMCE, a JavaScript WYSIWYG editor from Moxiecode Systems (http://tinymce.moxiecode.com/), to the blog and the wiki so staff would not have to learn blog and wiki rendering syntax. Navigational links back to the intranet homepage and the inclusion of the intranet banner served to better incorporate the tools into the intranet's overall context.

One disadvantage of open source tools is that the team sometimes felt it was operating in uncharted territory. The library Web manager made several contacts by e-mail and instant messaging with the authors of the tools to resolve issues that arose. Testing these tools was also an opportunity to begin documenting procedures for future staff training.

During the installation and refinement of the software packages, development of the site architecture of the redesigned intranet continued. Existing pages were converted to the new user interface. Staff members could monitor the progress via a link on the existing intranet homepage to the new site. The new site was unveiled in early 2009 (see Figure 2).

A number of ColdFusion elements and capabilities were used to incorporate and automate various features on the homepage:

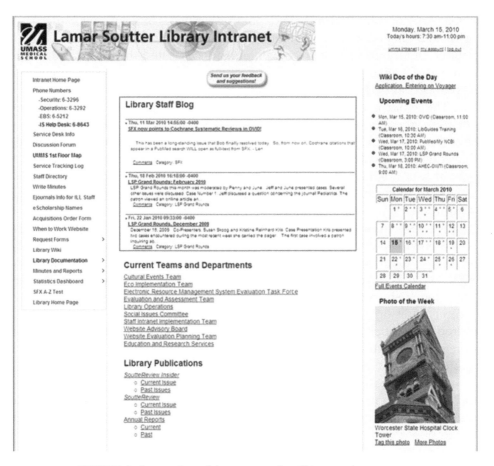

FIGURE 2 Screen shot of the renovated staff intranet home page.

- The left-hand menu is persistent throughout the intranet and is included by the ColdFusion cfinclude tag, making edits to the menu much easier to implement across all pages. Furthermore, the menu uses the cfmenu tag, which allows style-able dynamic submenus without having to script them in CSS or JavaScript.
- The prominent blog section in the center of the homepage lists the beginning text of the latest three postings with links to the full entry; they are also included on the homepage from the blog's RSS feed. The feed contents are retrieved using the ColdFusion cfhttp tag and parsed using the xmlparse() function.
- The "Wiki Doc of the Day" at the top of the right sidebar is included by a scheduled task in ColdFusion Administrator. The task is set to run a script that contains the ColdFusion randrange() function to generate a random integer. The random number is used to query the wiki data table

to retrieve the corresponding wiki entry, which is displayed on the intranet homepage.

- The "Upcoming Events" section is generated from a query of the calendar data table and uses the ColdFusion datecompare() function to display just the events in the next few days. Below that list is a thumbnail version of the full calendar, which uses small red asterisks to link to the information about an event. There is also a link to the full events calendar, which is an application from Advanced ColdFusion Professional Ben Nadel's Web site (http://www.bennadel.com).
- The photo collection is highlighted by the "Photo of the Week" and is included in a manner similar to the "Wiki Doc of the Day." Every Monday morning, a scheduled task selects a new photo and displays it on the homepage. A link to the full collection appears under the photo. All ColdFusion database queries on the homepage are cached to reduce the number of calls to the database.
- The "Today's Hours" feature on the upper right appears on every intranet page. It is included by a ColdFusion Component and is mirrored on the library's public Web site. Extended hours and holiday hours can be specified in an XML script.

TRAINING AND EVALUATION

Since the new interface and specialized tools were not yet available to the library staff, the team felt it was crucial to recommend in its report to library management the formation of a follow-up team to provide training and support. Staff buy-in was considered important for the successful use of the software packages, which could only happen if staff members felt confident enough to incorporate them into their workflow.

In March 2009, the Staff Intranet Implementation Team's term was extended so it could develop "train the trainer" sessions for selected library staff members. Instruction focused on the four specialized tools listed above. In preparation for the training, a manual for each tool was developed using the wiki and housed there. The team conducted training sessions in late April and early May 2009 for nine library staff members who were designated to train the staff in their departments.

At about this time, the team's life was extended through December 2009 to monitor and evaluate the use of the new tools and the redesigned intranet as a whole. After the initial training was completed, the team shifted its focus to gathering feedback from staff on the effectiveness and usefulness of the renovated intranet. Surveys, usability tests, follow-up meetings with the nine staff trainers, and a log of staff-generated errors were all suggested and implemented.

Another survey, sent in August 2009, was completed by 24 library staff members (the same return rate as the June 2008 survey). The first question was the same as in the 2008 survey, asking the average number of times per week the staff member logged into the intranet. This time only five respondents chose one to two times per week, while sixteen indicated they logged in at least five times per week, suggesting a greater interest in the new staff intranet.

The survey also included sections devoted to each of the four software tools, asking staff to rate each tool's ease of use and to answer questions about how the tool had been used. The wiki received the lowest average ratings for ease of use of the four applications. Responses for the other tools suggested a lower level of usage than the wiki, as many respondents chose the "N/A" option for many questions related to the blog, discussion forum, and photo collection. The responses to the question "Please state the reason(s) you don't use the [tool]" indicated that staff members were not using the tools because of lack of time or lack of training rather than because of technical problems with the respective applications. This supports O'Brien and Wisbey's emphasis on the "soft aspect" of the intranet (2008, 29). The team followed up with some one-on-one instruction and further discussions with the trainers.

The team also conducted usability testing of the intranet beginning in late August 2009, asking staff members who had undergone training in April and May to participate. The tests were a combination of task performance ob-servation and informal interview. Consistent with the survey results, usability testing indicated that the wiki was again the most difficult tool to use.

Some improvements to the usability of the tools were made based on this testing. In the wiki, for example, navigational enhancements were made, and the instruction manual was given more prominence. Also, the "password reminder" feature in the discussion forum was modified to ask for e-mail ad-dress rather than username. The library Web manager was able to implement this change after more contact with the forum developer.

DISCUSSION

Considering the relatively brief period of time that has passed between the first team meeting in March 2008 and the present, team members feel the newly renovated intranet, with the four tools in place, has already addressed several parts of the library strategic plan. Despite some usability issues, the wiki is already serving as a growing "central repository of current and archived library-wide policies and procedures" and is allowing library staff to "actively participate in collaborative efforts." The blog is helping to "com-municate to all staff new products and services at the library," while the discussion forum is offering "new ways for staff to provide input on new and/or old services, policies, procedures and how they can be improved" (Lamar Soutter Library 2006).

A new, more robust calendar application that supports setting meeting recurrence and multiple display options (i.e., day, week, month, and year) has been incorporated. The Web manager has added the capability to include meeting room locations, customized the display options to include a printable calendar for posting on the library's computer classroom door, and is currently adding e-mail notification to the appropriate staff when new events are posted. Another desirable feature that has yet to be planned is an intranet-wide search function.

In implementing the software tools, some unique challenges had to be overcome. As mentioned above, two tools require the Model-Glue framework, which also had to be installed on the library Web server. Each tool also has its own authentication system, which had to be either bypassed or modified to alleviate the need for multiple staff logins.

Some tools, such as the blog and the photo collection, were developed as applications for the public Internet. As such, the administrative modules are well hidden and secured. In the staff intranet's implementation, however, the team needed to make the admin layer more visible, so links were made that allow all library staff access to upload and manage images and to author blog postings.

Some desired changes to the tools could not be made because doing so would break the entire application. Other modifications sometimes led to loss of native functionality. For instance, the blog in its out-of-the-box configuration supports image uploading into postings. The addition of the TinyMCE toolbar, however, mysteriously deactivated this capability. This problem is still unresolved as of this writing.

It may be premature to assess what works well and what does not work as well on the intranet. While the wiki seems to be the source of most troublesome issues, it is also the most-used of the new tools available to staff. To date, there are 285 pages on the intranet wiki. Until other tools are used more frequently, the team may not be able to determine if they, too, will become problematic.

In retrospect, the team might have been able to achieve better buy-in for the wiki if there had been more time to educate library staff on what a wiki is and how it could be useful for their work. Team members were aware of an experience gap, where some staff members were quite adept at using a certain wiki product such as MediaWiki or Wetpaint, while others had no experience at all with any wiki. More evenly distributed training may have alleviated this situation. Team members have held follow-up training sessions with individual library staff, the effectiveness of which has yet to be evaluated.

Looking ahead, there are some unresolved questions to consider. Is the renovated staff intranet, particularly its new tools, saving staff time and meeting their needs? Who is responsible for promoting usage of the intranet tools? If a tool is getting little usage, does that constitute a failure of the team to accurately appraise staff needs, or does the problem lie with the tool itself? Will future iterations of the intranet necessitate an entirely different platform than ColdFusion?

On December 31, 2009, the team submitted its final report to library management, which included recommendations for future oversight and training for the intranet. At the time of this writing, library management is considering the next steps for the intranet.

CONCLUSION

From the beginning, the library's intranet team considered solutions that would hopefully be a good fit for the library's specific needs. The team had the dual task of redesigning the intranet's outdated user interface and considering new tools to include for staff productivity. Given the resources of time, existing technology, and budget available to the team, many decisions had to be made quickly. The question of retooling the intranet into another scripting language had to be balanced against the amount of time available. At the same time, the renovated staff intranet has shown potential in furthering some of the goals of the library strategic plan.

ACKNOWLEDGMENTS

The authors would like to thank Raymond Camden (author of Canvas Cold-Fusion Wiki, BlogCFC, and Galleon ColdFusion Forums) and Seth Duffey (author of CFCPhotoBlog) for their assistance in extending the four ColdFusion software applications mentioned in this article. They would also like to thank Jane Fama, associate director for Library Operations, for her helpful suggestions in preparing this manuscript.

REFERENCES

Cotter, Lisa, Larnich Harije, and Suzanne Lewis. 2006. Adding SPICE to a library intranet site: A recipe to enhance usability. *Evidence Based Library and Information Practice* 1(1): 3–25. http://ejournals.library.ualberta.ca/index.php/EBLIP/article/view/11/81 (accessed October 9, 2009).

Fichter, Darlene. 2005. Intranets, wikis, blikis, and collaborative working. *Online* 29(5): 47–50.

———. 2006a. Making your intranet live up to its potential. *Online* 30(1; January/February): 51–53.

————. 2006b. Using contextual inquiry to build a better intranet. *Online* 30(5): 46–48.

Fichter, Darlene, and Jeff Wisniewski. 2008. Wiki while you work. *Online* 32(3; May): 55–57.

Glogowski, Joel, and Sarah Steiner. 2008. The life of a wiki: How Georgia State University library's wiki enhances content currency and employee collaboration. *Internet Reference Services Quarterly* 13(1): 87–98.

Kennedy, Mary Lee, and Jane Dysart. 2007. *Intranets for info pros*. Medford, NJ: Information Today.

Lamar Soutter Library, University of Massachusetts Medical School. 2006. Strategic plan 2006–2009. http://library.umassmed.edu/strat_plan_apr06.pdf (accessed October 9, 2009).

————. 2008a. Teams, task forces, and committees—staff intranet implementation team. http://library.umassmed.edu/team_details.cfm?team=staff_intr_impl08 (accessed October 27, 2009).

————. 2008b. Teams, task forces, and committees—staff intranet team. http://library.umassmed.edu/team_details.cfm?team=staff_intr08 (accessed October 9, 2009).

Langley, Nick. 2007. ColdFusion offers a short curve to Web development. *ComputerWeekly.com*, June 11. http://www.computerweekly.com/Articles/2007/06/11/224682/coldfusion-offers-a-short-curve-to-web-development.htm (accessed October 29, 2009).

Martini, Antonella, Mariano Corso, and Luisa Pellegrini. 2009. An empirical roadmap for intranet evolution. *International Journal of Information Management* 29(4): 295–308.

Model-Glue Team. 2009. The model-glue framework. http://www.model-glue.com/ (accessed October 26, 2009).

Nielsen, Jakob. 2009. Discount usability: 20 years. *Jakob Nielsen's Alertbox*. http://www.useit.com/alertbox/discount-usability.html (accessed October 28, 2009).

O'Brien, Mel, and Jillian Wisbey. 2008. Building a dynamic online learning and community environment. *Access* 22(3; September): 29–35.

Robbins, Sarah, Debra Engel, and James Bierman. 2006. Using the library intranet to manage Web content. *Library Hi Tech* 24(2): 261–272.

For Better or Worse: Using Wikis and Blogs for Staff Communication in an Academic Library

KRISTEN COSTELLO and DARCY DEL BOSQUE

University Libraries, University of Nevada, Las Vegas, Nevada, USA

This case study from the University of Nevada, Las Vegas, University Libraries, which has one main library, three branches, and more than 110 staff, illustrates one approach to using new technologies as additional methods for internal communication. At large academic libraries, communication within the organization can be challenging. The potential that Web 2.0 tools have to increase opportunities for communication and collaboration is one reason internal staff wiki and blogs were implemented at the University Libraries. The staff wiki is predominantly used to archive committee meeting minutes, policies and procedures, and departmental information, while blogs are used mainly for news items and departmental updates. The University of Nevada, Las Vegas, library staff were surveyed to assess the changes in communication after the implementation of blogs and an internal wiki. The authors theorized that Web 2.0 technologies would reduce barriers and improve communication. Results indicated an overall improvement in internal staff communication after the implementation of the staff wiki; however, no change was noted with blogs. Findings also showed several challenges for the future, including the need for additional training with the tools and a desire for more regular postings to the blogs. A major test for the future is ensuring that these new Web 2.0 technologies become more integrated into staff workflows so the technologies will be more readily adopted by library staff as additional communication channels.

Employees generally want to be informed about their organizations and are often receptive to improvements in communication. Web 2.0 tools, which have emerged in the last decade, offer one potential solution to communication issues within organizations. These tools allow staff to communicate with each other in new ways, enhancing collaboration, knowledge sharing, and communication, while remaining easy to access and use. Yet despite their promise, many Web 2.0 tools have not been systematically adopted by libraries. This article aims to provide background on how two of those tools, blogs and wikis, have been implemented to facilitate internal communication at a large academic library. By reviewing the literature and through a case study of the University of Nevada, Las Vegas (UNLV), University Libraries, the potential pitfalls and successes of blogs and wikis used for internal communication are discussed. This study began an assessment of the implementation outcomes by surveying staff about their perceptions of the changes in communication after the implementation of blogs and wikis. Suggestions for future improvements are also provided.

LITERATURE REVIEW

This research focuses on blogs and wikis, which are two commonly used Web 2.0 tools in libraries. Literature concerning the general topic of Web 2.0 usage in libraries is widely published. However, to uncover information concerning library use of Web 2.0 tools specifically for internal communication, one must examine each tool individually.

Wikis

The collaborative nature of wikis and their ability to allow multiple people to edit them have made wikis ideal for communication within organizations. However, only a small subset of the literature about wikis speaks to this. Two studies have explored the systematic adoption of wikis in libraries and touch on how they have been used for internal communication. Samuel Kai-Wah Chu's (2009) article, "Using Wikis in Academic Libraries," explored the use of wikis at 60 university libraries. He found the most popular reason cited for the use of wikis was to improve the sharing of information between librarians (172), which illustrates that libraries do see a use for Web 2.0 technologies for enhancing internal communication. Matthew M. Bejune (2007) also investigated the use of wikis in libraries. He located and categorized

33 library wikis, finding that they were used for collaboration among library staff 31.4 percent of the time (Bejune 2007, 33).

Many case studies have been written about implementing wikis for use in internal communication. One of the first, written by Rob Withers (2005), discussed a successful implementation of a wiki to share information among desk staff at his library. Library staff valued the wiki for its ability to "be continuously updated and viewed by all staff members; typographical errors, rapidly changing availability of online services, and new information can all be reflected in entries in a timely fashion" (777). Nancy T. Lombardo, Allyson Mower, and Mary M. McFarland analyzed the use of a wiki at the Spencer S. Eccles Health Sciences Library at the University of Utah for a variety of internal communication needs, including grant proposals, committee work, and development of a library strategic plan, and as a systems department documentation and communication forum (2008, 130). The article discussed the pros and cons of different wiki types and the success and failure of various wiki projects, concluding as "more emphasis is placed on teams working collaboratively, these social networking tools will be instrumental in facilitating this work environment" (144).

Jon Haupt (2007) wrote about the process of implementing a wiki at the Iowa State University Library. Although many ideas for the content of the wiki were proposed, the internal faculty research resources pages were chosen as a pilot for the project. The experiences of the implementation were shared "to assure doubtful librarians that creating a useful wiki is not only possible, but within reach" (91). Joel Glogowski and Sarah Steiner (2008) wrote about the wikis at Georgia State University Library, which were implemented as early as 2003. They concluded that one of the primary roles their wikis served was with internal communication, noting, "The use of the wiki has spread to almost all of the library's departments and has helped staff members from different departments to see more clearly where their policies and concerns overlap" (95).

Constance Wiebrands (2006) provided a case study from the Curtin University Library in Perth, Australia. She discussed how a particular wiki software was chosen and implemented and commented on some of the uses for the wiki, including creating and documenting policy statements and guidelines, serving as an electronic notebook, and functioning as a knowledge base. She acknowledged both positive and negative outcomes for the project but said, "The wiki is worth investigating as a tool for the library, as it can make collaboration more efficient and more effective. The fact that material on the wiki is so easy to edit means that users are more likely to develop a sense of ownership and responsibility and are more inclined to keep material on the wiki current" (8). The University of Houston Music Library also implemented a wiki to use for internal communication. It began as a replacement for the library's policies and procedures manual but expanded to include training for student workers, a place to record and discuss problems with daily operations, and a location to store data (such as gate count statistics). Tammy Ravas (2008) noted, "While the wiki was a success in some areas, challenges surfaced as well" (50). Anne Welsh (2007) discussed using wikis internally, specifically for procedures and training. She mentioned the benefits of implementing a wiki and provided ten tips for a successful procedures wiki. Like others, she cautions that wikis will not be the perfect solution, saying, "It's only a wiki, and it's only one part of a knowledge-sharing culture" (29). Ellie Dworak and Keven Jeffery (2009) included an evaluation component in their article about San Diego State University Library switching to a wiki for an intranet. They concluded that one of the primary benefits of the wiki was the increased awareness of staff about the ability to update their own content (409).

Blogs

Like wikis, blogs are used for a variety of purposes beyond internal communication, including disseminating news and providing information for a particular user group, for specific projects, or for marketing or promoting resources or events. Michael Stephens's (2006) chapter on blogs in the book *Web 2.0 & Libraries: Best Practices for Social Software* provided an in-depth overview of what blogs are, how they can be used in libraries, and what the steps are for implementation. He also discussed using blogs for internal communication, noting, "Internal blogging can replace e-mail in many instances, bulletin-board postings, and even some meetings!" (21). He did note that not all blogs have been successful, citing staff buy-in as an essential component (22).

The popularity of blogs in libraries began in the mid-2000s. Before then, relatively few libraries had adopted them; Laurel A. Clyde's study on blogs (2004) showed that in 2003, only one library was using a blog for internal communication (186). Rachel Singer Gordon and Michael Stephens (2006) promoted using blogs for internal communication, saying, "You'll benefit from improved communication, practice with technology, and experience using social software" (50). They wrote about the ease of setting up a blog for a library, emphasizing planning and promotion to make blogging for internal communication successful.

Several authors reflected on the planning and support necessary to make a blog successful. Alison McIntyre and Janette Nicolle (2008) described two case studies on blogs at the University of Canterbury Library, one of which illustrated the implementation of a blog to solve internal communication problems. The authors found the internal blog project to be successful, saying the blog "has more than met our expectations in terms of cost and convenience and has improved communication of essential information across the library system" (686). Tania Bardyn (2009) provided five factors needed for the successful implementation of blogs in libraries, observing libraries cannot just establish a blog and "count on it being a booming business" (12). Susan Leandri (2007) also provided a set of best practices libraries should follow when implementing blogs. She advocated for using internal blogs, but she cautioned, "To be successful, they must provide value to the individual employee, facilitate finding and contacting other similarly minded individuals, and be easy to access, read and browse" (16). Leandri also suggested having a librarian in charge of internal blogs to ensure regular maintenance (17). Joanna Blair and Cathy Cranston (2006) stated, "Planning is paramount and should be the first step toward creating a thriving and long-lasting blog" (10). They reviewed the implementation of blogs at their own library and recommended steps for others to take when creating blogs.

The literature clearly indicates the potential for blogs and wikis to improve internal communication within a library organization exists. However, it also makes clear that simply using new technologies will not automatically improve existing communication problems. This case study assesses the implementation of blogs and wikis at a large academic library for the improvement of internal communication. Unlike earlier investigations, this study focuses on staff perceptions of how the implementation of blogs and wikis have affected communication within the organization.

BACKGROUND

The UNLV University Libraries is a large academic library with a main library and three branches. The libraries served a student population of 28,605 during the fall 2008 semester. Seventy-seven percent of its students are undergraduates. The total headcount for UNLV employees is 3,168, with 110 being University Libraries staff, not including part-time and student workers (UNLV 2008).

Establishing good communication is essential for any organization to function effectively. Given the size of the UNLV library staff, the four separate locations, and the large, diverse student population, the communication process can potentially break down at any point. Knowing the importance of good communication to the organization, the library administration has made a commitment, via the strategic plan (UNLV 2009), to promote "open, clear, and honest communication at all levels" (n.p.). Despite these intentions, an employment satisfaction survey conducted in 2008 showed that communication was an area in which staff felt a negative impact, although it had seen some improvement from the previous year. The researchers were curious to know if the recent implementation of wikis and blogs had been a factor in the improvement.

In addition to encouraging effective communication throughout all levels of the organization, the UNLV University Libraries encourages and supports innovation and the use of new technologies, including Web 2.0, by staff. Unlike in business settings, where profits are the bottom line, the libraries offer an environment that is open to innovation through experimentation. In striving to become a library of the future, the libraries have implemented numerous Web 2.0 projects over the past decade. Among these innovations have been blogs, wikis, Facebook, Twitter, Flickr, and instant messaging. Many of these technologies, including blogs and wikis, began as informal projects that were later expanded and formally adopted by the libraries or discontinued because of poor results.

IMPLEMENTATION OF BLOGS

There was no formal project to establish blogs at UNW, but interested librarians were allowed to experiment with creating and publishing blogs. In 2004, the medical/health sciences librarian was the first person to create a public blog, which was maintained using Blogger (http://www.blogger.com). Her interest in blog technology was as an alternative outreach method with faculty, because she considered newsletters to be old fashioned, and faculty complained of getting too much e-mail. The Research and Information (R&I) Department was another early adopter of blogs. The R&I blog was intended to be used internally by reference desk staff to share information. Several staff members could post on the blog, and entries usually covered topics and updates important to reference desk staff, such as an answer to a question that multiple students were asking for an assignment. Although the rest of the staff did not have permission to post entries, they did have the ability to comment on entries. Initially the blog flourished, but after several of the more enthusiastic contributors to the blog left the organization, the blog became stagnant. The R&I blog has been retired because of low usage, and some of the information that used to be stored there has been moved to the staff wiki.

The libraries host 26 blogs; most of them are available to the public, although seven are accessible by staff only. Of the seven internal blogs, only three have library-wide readership appeal ("The Dean's Blog," "UNLV's Innovative Integrated Library System Blog," and the "Assessment Blog"). The other four blogs target either specific user types (like the "Student Assistant Blog") or specific divisions, branches, or units (like the "Architecture Studies Library Staff Notes Blog"). Of the public blogs, the "Library News" blog (http://blogs.library.unlv.edu/newsblog) has the widest readership because of its prominent location on the home page.

In May 2006, the libraries migrated to Moveable Type (http://www.movabletype.com) software, which the libraries still use. All blogs have the same branded look, but blog owners can choose the blog name and various features. An entry on the staff wiki provides blog policy information and links to all currently available blogs.

Routine training and troubleshooting for blogs developed as they were adopted as part of the libraries' communication structure. The Libraries Technologies Division provides technical support for blogs, including the creation of accounts. Any library staff member can request a work-related blog by completing a form available on the staff wiki. The Web and Digitization Unit (WDS) also provides support for blogs through training, which has typically been one-on-one. Recently, the libraries introduced a staff training program, which includes a "Get Started on Blogging" mini-workshop. In addition to staff training, the WDS encourages staff to use feed readers so they can be notified when public blogs have been updated. The WDS has also created an e-mail notification system for internal blogs, which some feed readers cannot access.

IMPLEMENTATION OF WIKIS

An internal staff wiki was introduced in May 2007 as a possible replacement for the staff intranet, which was a password-protected set of Web pages stored on the libraries' Web server. The decision to move to a wiki instead of continuing to host the intranet came from a working group, but it was also heavily influenced by experimentation with wikis from the Libraries Technology Division and the Web Management Committee and by individual liaisons who were making use of freely available hosted wikis for some of their work. The UNLV Libraries chose MediaWiki (http://www.mediawiki. org/wiki/MediaWiki), the same software that Wikipedia uses. VbGORE (http://www.vbgore.com/Main_Page) created a new skin to keep the look and feel of the wiki similar to the old intranet. There is an A–Z list of topics on the front page, which highlights certain categories of information. Information from the old staff intranet was transferred to the staff wiki, and blank template pages were created for all standing committees.

Although committees, departments, and divisions were all strongly encouraged to use the staff wiki to post minutes, policies, and other information, there were a few challenges. Contributions to the wiki got off to a slow start, but frequent use by certain committees helped staff to start relying on the wiki to find and post information. Another hurdle was that wiki markup language was required to create pages. Wiki markup is a simplified version of HTML; however, it was still complicated enough to cause some confusion and apprehension among staff. To ease this technical hurdle, the FCKeditor extension was added (http://www.mediawiki.org/wiki/Extension:FCKeditor_(Official)). It is a WYSIWYG editor that gives staff a choice between using a word-processor-like editor or the wiki markup. This switch helped to get more content added to the wiki. Gradually, as these challenges were addressed, more people began to adopt the wiki.

Training was another opportunity to get people comfortable using the wiki. There were two all-staff wiki training sessions on how to create and edit content. The training sessions included hands-on experience with a training wiki. The training wiki was set up so staff would have an environment in which to experiment and practice without the fear of breaking something.

A wiki policy and FAQ page were posted on the wiki to provide staff with guidelines and tips for page creation. Technical issues and questions, as well as any additional training, are handled by the chair of the Staff Web Working Group.

During the implementation of both blogs and wikis, there was an understanding within the libraries that encouragement and training would be needed to make the adoption successful. The dean showed her support for the transition by requiring that certain information be housed on the staff wiki and by creating her own internal blog to share information with staff. Despite the training and encouragement to use these new Web 2.0 tools, there still appears to be a reluctance and apprehension to use them.

RESEARCH PROBLEM

This study aims to uncover the perceptions of staff concerning the staff wiki and blogs. A survey was used to determine if these new technologies have been helpful in facilitating communication in the organization and to uncover how these tools might be improved in the future. Previous staff surveys at the UNLV Libraries have identified communication issues within the organization. Although these issues have been addressed in various ways, the organization has not undertaken an investigation into currently used communication channels. Furthermore, no formal assessment has been done for blogs and the staff wiki since their implementation. It is theorized that the Web 2.0 technologies employed by the libraries have improved internal staff communication, but the reality remained unclear. The researchers wanted to gather the perceptions of all library staff toward a variety of communication channels, including the staff wiki and blogs. This method of assessment was chosen because the UNLV Libraries have a sizeable staff working various schedules and it was the most efficient method to collect the data and reach the widest representation of staff members.

DATA COLLECTION

A survey was created to gather information about staff perceptions of the libraries' communication channels, with several questions focused specifically on the effectiveness of blogs and the staff wiki (see Appendix 1). The survey was created using SurveyMonkey (http://www.surveymonkey.com). The survey consisted of 21 questions, which were primarily multiple-choice questions, with an option to type in comments. The first two questions on the survey were required to comply with the institution's Office for the Protection of Research Subjects informed consent policy. A link to the survey was e-mailed to all library employees, asking them to participate. The Web survey afforded the respondents privacy and anonymity, and they could withdraw from the survey at any point. The survey was available to staff over a two-week period. The staff employee count was 110 during the surveyed period. Forty-four employees began taking the survey, although not every respondent answered every question; 38 employees completed the survey, for a completion rate of 86.4 percent.

SURVEY RESULTS

The survey responses were collected and analyzed. The survey first discussed five communication channels commonly used in the libraries and then gathered additional feedback specifically about blogs and wikis. The five communication channels were e-mail, the networked shared drive (a shared space where files can be stored in folders and accessed only by people with the appropriate authorization), meetings, the staff wiki, and blogs. The first question in the survey addressed various communication channels used by library staff to share information with each other. E-mail was the predominant method of choice, with 100 percent of respondents using e-mail to send and receive information. Meetings (85 percent) and the staff wiki (82.5 percent) were the second and third most popular methods; blogs were the least used method at 52.5 percent.

What was surprising is that 94.7 percent of the staff surveyed chose e-mail as their preferred method of staff communication. The wiki followed at 23 percent, meetings at 18.4 percent, and the blogs at only 7.9 percent (see Figure 1). To allow staff to indicate all preferred methods of communication, more than one response was allowed. One staff member mentioned she would like to be notified via e-mail when something is posted on the wiki, which may indicate that without a built-in notification system, staff do not think to check the wiki for updated information. Another stated, "It seems silly to send an e-mail telling people that I posted something [on the blog]—but that's the only way I am sure people see it." Many comments mentioned that meetings are a preferred method, but it is interesting to note that only seven respondents preferred meetings over e-mail.

E-mail ranked as the easiest method to access (71.1 percent) and with which to post information (78.9 percent). Discrepancies were revealed when comparing ease of access to ease of posting or adding content among other communication channels. The staff wiki was the second easiest method to access, but it was in third place when staff wanted to actually add content. Libraries staff preferred meetings over blogs or the networked share drive when accessing information (see Figure 2). One staff member said the telephone is also easy when seeking information, and another remarked all the methods are equally easy with the exception of the dean's blog, which is

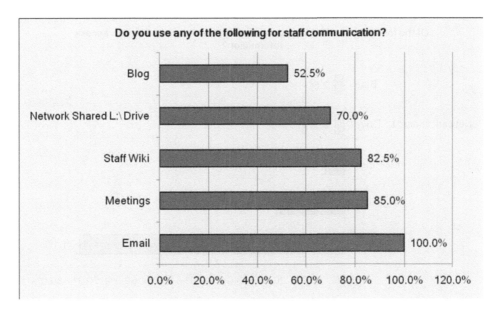

FIGURE 1 Types of staff communication.

restricted by IP address. The network shared drive was perceived as the second easiest method for posting information, while no staff member picked blogs as the easiest method for adding information (see Figure 3). A telling comment about posting information was "Just because it's easiest to post doesn't make it the most effective!"

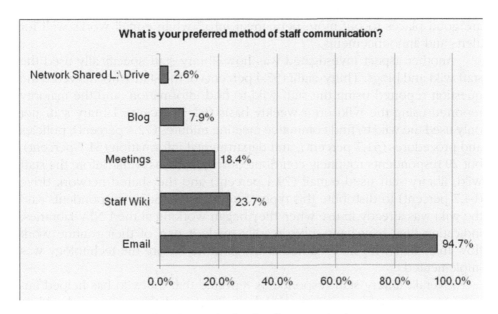

FIGURE 2 Methods of staff communication.

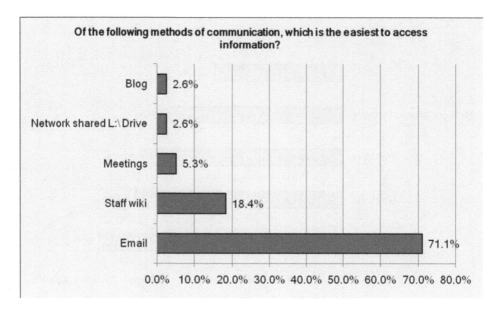

FIGURE 3 Easiest methods of communication.

The majority of library staff considered e-mail the most effective communication method. However, as one respondent remarked, it is effective only "if the target audience actually reads the e-mail message." No one selected the network share drive as an effective communication method. Although the effectiveness depends on the type of information that is retrieved and conveyed, one person commented, "The wiki and the [network shared drive] are good places to put more permanent info," while e-mail works well for alerts and announcements.

Another aspect investigated was how library staff specifically used the staff wiki and blogs. Thirty-eight (97.4 percent) of the staff who answered the question reported using the staff wiki to find information, and the majority reported using the wiki on a weekly basis (62.5 percent). Library staff not only used the wiki to find committee meeting minutes (72.4 percent), policies and procedures (51.7 percent), and departmental information (51.7 percent), but 29 respondents routinely contributed to the wiki as well. Before the staff wiki, library staff used e-mail (79.4 percent) and the shared network drive (64.7 percent) to distribute this type of information. Some respondents said the wiki was already in use when they began working at the UNLV Libraries, indicating they may have more readily made it part of their routine work flow than staff who had worked at the libraries before the technology was implemented.

Overall, library staff respondents reported that the wiki has helped improve internal staff communication but recognized that using and adding content to the wiki takes effort. There were multiple comments about remote access issues with the wiki; library staff must still install virtual private network (VPN) software and log in before they can get to the wiki when working from home or while out of town. Some staff members said the A–Z index is helpful, while others complained it is "hard to find things. Nothing is where I think it should be." Many were glad there is finally a central location for library information. Comments from staff members shared a common theme: the wiki is a great place to look for information, but they do not feel they are proficient in adding content, despite the libraries' training sessions.

The library blogs are clearly an underused resource. Only 21.1 percent of the staff surveyed said they use the blogs to find information. The majority of respondents (31.6 percent) reads a library-related blog only every few months, and some never do (15.8 percent). Most of the respondents (73.7 percent) do not add content, nor do they comment to any library blogs. Of the 7.9 percent of the staff who do write library blogs, content posted is equally distributed among news information and departmental procedures (60 percent).

When library personnel were asked how information was shared before the blog was created, their answers differed from the question on how information was shared before the wiki. Ninety-six percent of the staff surveyed answered that e-mail was the primary method of sharing information, whereas only 79.4 percent picked e-mail when they were asked the same question about the staff wiki. Not one person thought the blogs have greatly improved staff communication (see Figure 4). Perhaps the blogs need better marketing because many staff members forget the blogs. Blog authors

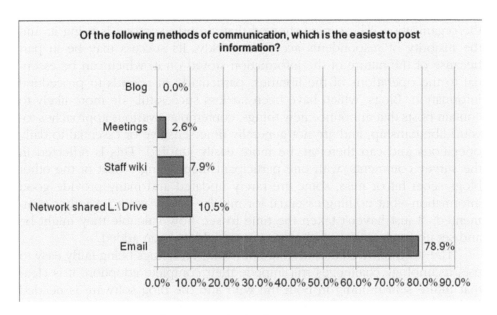

FIGURE 4 Easiest methods of posting communication.

are also frustrated because it is difficult to determine if their posts have any impact when comments are seldom or rarely made. Another person commented, "It gets overwhelming to keep up." Library blogs seem to be inconsistently used and referenced and do not seem to contribute to enhancing communication at the libraries.

CONCLUSIONS

Although the experiences of the University Libraries are unique to this organization, they do seem to reflect what has happened at other institutions. For instance, the University of Houston Music Library found the wiki pages updated most often were those that someone was required to update on a regular basis, while at the UNLV Libraries, the pages that were updated most frequently were committee pages, which also had a requirement for a minimum amount of information to be posted (Ravas 2008). Like Curtin University Library, UNLV staff found it difficult to work with the original wiki language, and an editor had to be added to make it easier to post information (Wiebrands 2006). Similar to a warning from Colorado State University Libraries, which stated, "Not all blogs will be wholeheartedly embraced, even with the best-laid plans," the libraries' blogs have struggled with creating a following (Blair and Cranston 2006, 54). It seems that simply implementing new technologies does not mean automatic adoption by staff; moreover, it takes a consistent effort of internal marketing and subtle reminders to get new technologies integrated into the workflow of the organization.

It is also notable that the staff wiki has had a great deal of success in the organization. The survey showed that almost everyone is using it, and the majority of respondents access it weekly. Its success may be in part because of the nature of the information stored on it, which can be essential to the operations of the libraries, particularly in regards to procedural information. Blogs, which have been far less successful, are more likely to contain posts that announce new things, contemplate various approaches toward librarianship, and are not generally time sensitive or essential to daily operations and can therefore be more easily ignored. This is reflected in the survey comments, with one participant mentioning, "Most of the other blogs seem hit or miss, some are rarely updated and many provide good information—but nothing essential for my day-to-day work." Another commented, "I just haven't taken the time to see how valuable they might be and set up feeds to know when new material has been added."

The study showed that despite both wikis and blogs being fairly easy to use, technology challenges still impede their complete adoption. It is clear that future staff training in both the wiki and the blog software is needed and that the training should be repeated at various intervals to accommodate new employees or employees who use the applications very rarely. Staff were much more comfortable using blogs and wikis to receive information than to post it, which could be in part because of the technological obstacles of having to set up accounts to use each system and with overcoming the learning curve of how each system works. Another technological frustration noted by many survey respondents was the inability to easily access the staff wiki and the internal library blogs (such as the dean's blog) when outside the library network.

Many survey respondents indicated their preferred method of communication changed depending on the situation, an indication that the libraries should support multiple channels of communication. For example, one person mentioned that a combination of communication channels was needed based on the type of information needing to be retrieved and conveyed, providing the following examples: "Meeting minutes? Wiki. Quick question without a real time requirement? E-mail. Need to hammer out details and timeline of a plan? Meeting." The wiki and blogs add two new tools to help bridge the gap in communication in a large academic organization. Although there are clearly steps that need to be taken in the future to improve the integration of the staff wiki and blogs into the workflow of library employees, the success of the wiki demonstrates that staff recognize the benefits these new technologies hold.

Web 2.0 technologies are not new to the UNLV University Libraries. Library blogs have been in use at the libraries for more than five years, and a staff wiki has been in place for two years. Surprisingly, e-mail is still the most preferred communication method at the UNLV Libraries. Even within a culture that encourages staff to embrace and experiment new technology, library staff are slow to consistently use and integrate wikis and blogs into their everyday work routine.

REFERENCES

Bardyn, Tania P. 2009. Library blogs: What's most important for success within the enterprise? *Computers in Libraries* 29(6): 12–16.

Bejune, Matthew M. 2007. Wikis in libraries. *Information Technology and Libraries* 26(3): 26–38.

Blair, Joanna, and Cathy Cranston. 2006. Preparing for the birth of our library BLOG. *Computers in Libraries* 26(2): 10–13, 54.

Clyde, Laurel A. 2004. Library Weblogs. *Library Management* 25(4/5): 183–189.

Dworak, Ellie, and Keven Jeffery. 2009. Wiki to the rescue: Creating a more dynamic intranet. *Library Hi Tech* 27(3): 403–410.

Glogowski, Joel, and Sarah Steiner. 2008. The life of a wiki: How Georgia State University Library's wiki enhances content currency and employee collaboration. *Internet References Services Quarterly* 13(1): 87–98.

Gordon, Rachel Singer, and Michael Stephens. 2006. Tech tips for every librarian: How and why to try a blog for staff communication. *Computers in Libraries* 26(2): 50–51.

Haupt, Jon. 2007. From zero to wiki. *Journal of Web Librarianship* 1(1): 77–92.

Kai-Wah Chu, Samuel. 2009. Using wikis in academic libraries. *The Journal of Academic Librarianship* 35(2): 170–176.

Leandri, Susan. 2007. Five ways to improve your corporate blogs. *Information Outlook* 11(1): 14–18.

Lombardo, Nancy T., Allyson Mower, and Mary M. McFarland. 2008. Putting wikis to work in libraries. *Medical Reference Services Quarterly* 27(2): 129–145.

McIntyre, Alison, and Jannette Nicolle. 2008. Biblioblogging: Blogs for library communication. *The Electronic Library* 26(5): 683–694.

Ravas, Tammy. 2008. Not just a policies and procedures manual anymore: The University of Houston Music Library manual wiki. *Notes* 65(1): 38–52.

Stephens, Michael. 2006. Web 2.0 & libraries: Best practices for social software. *Library Technology Reports* 42(4): 6–66.

University of Nevada Las Vegas. 2008. Facts and stats. http://www.unlv.edu/about/facts.html (accessed May 17, 2010).

University of Nevada Las Vegas University Libraries. 2009. UNLV Libraries strategic plan 2009–2011. http://www.library.unlv.edu/about/strategic_plan09-11.pdf (accessed May 17, 2010).

Welsh, Anne. 2007. Internal wikis for procedures and training: From tacit knowledge to self-guided learning. *Online* 31(6): 26–29.

Wiebrands, Constance. 2006. Collaboration and communication via wiki: The experience of Curtin University Library and information service. Paper presented at Australian Library and Information Association 2006 Biennial Conference, September 19–22, in Perth, Australia. http://eprints.rclis.org/7481/ (accessed September 4, 2009).

Withers, Rob. 2005. Something wiki this way comes. *College and Research Libraries News* 66(11): 775–777.

APPENDIX A: SURVEY QUESTIONS

Communication

1. Do you use any of the following for staff communication?
   a. E-mail
   b. Network shared L:\ drive
   c. Meetings
   d. Staff wiki
   e. Blog

2. What is your preferred method of staff communication?
   a. E-mail
   b. Network shared L:\ drive
   c. Meetings
   d. Staff wiki
   e. Blog
   f. Other

3. Of the following methods of communication, which is the easiest to access information?
    a. E-mail
    b. Network shared L:\ drive
    c. Meetings
    d. Staff wiki
    e. Blog
    f. Other
4. Of the following methods of communication, which is the easiest to post information?
    a. E-mail
    b. Network shared L:\ drive
    c. Meetings
    d. Staff wiki
    e. Blog
    f. Other
5. Overall which of the following methods of communication, which is the most effective?
    a. E-mail
    b. Network shared L:\ drive
    c. Meetings
    d. Staff wiki
    e. Blog
    f. Other

Wikis

1. How often do you use the staff wiki?
    a. Daily
    b. Weekly
    c. Monthly
    d. Every few months
    e. Never
2. Do you use the staff wiki to find information?
    a. Yes
    b. No
3. Do you contribute (add content) to the staff wiki?
    a. Yes
    b. No
4. What types of information are you contributing to the wiki?
    a. Committee meeting minutes
    b. Policies and procedures
    c. Department information

5. How was information shared before the staff wiki?
   a. Intranet (Web pages)
   b. E-mail
   c. UNLV Libraries Web site
   d. Shared network L:\ drive
   e. Other
6. Since the implementation of the wiki, communication has
   a. Greatly improved
   b. Improved
   c. No change
   d. Declined
   e. Greatly declined
7. Please provide any additional comments about the staff wiki.

Blogs

1. How often do you read a library blog?
   a. Daily
   b. Weekly
   c. Monthly
   d. Every few months
   e. Never
2. Do you use a library blog to find information?
   a. Yes
   b. No
3. Do you contribute (add content) to a library blog?
   a. Yes
   b. No
4. What types of information are you contributing to a library blog?
   a. News items
   b. Departmental updates
   c. Policies and procedures
   d. New services
   e. New technologies
   f. Information for patrons
   g. Other
5. How was information shared before the blog?
   a. Intranet (Web pages)
   b. E-mail
   c. UNLV Libraries Web site
   d. Shared network L:\ drive
   e. Other

6. Since the implementation of the blog, communication has
   a. Greatly improved
   b. Improved
   c. No change
   d. Declined
   e. Greatly declined
7. Please provide any additional comments about the blogs.

When the New Application Smell Is Gone: Traditional Intranet Best Practices and Existing Web 2.0 Intranet Infrastructures

BECKY YOOSE

Technical Services Department, Miami University Libraries, Oxford, Ohio, USA

With the growth of Web 2.0 library intranets in recent years, many libraries are leaving behind legacy, first-generation intranets. As Web 2.0 intranets multiply and mature, how will traditional intranet best practices—especially in the areas of planning, implementation, and evaluation—translate into an existing Web 2.0 intranet infrastructure? This article explores traditional intranet theories and best practices in relation to the two generations of the Web 2.0 intranet at the Technical Services Department at the Miami University Libraries. The case study explores the evaluation of the first-generation Web 2.0 intranet (implemented in 2005) and the planning and implementation of the second-generation Web 2.0 intranet in 2008. While the technologies are different, the case study shows many of the best practices established for traditional intranets still hold true for the Web 2.0 intranets in the case study. Following many of the traditional best practices helped the second Web 2.0 intranet to succeed, while not following established practices hurt the first Web 2.0 intranet's ability to meet departmental expectations of information access and information currency. Nonetheless, there are issues specific to Web 2.0 intranets that are not covered in existing best practices. More input is needed before establishing Web 2.0-specific intranet best practices.

In its relatively short period of existence, concepts and technologies surrounding Web 2.0 have made staggering changes in how libraries serve their customers. Libraries use Web 2.0 applications for a wide range of purposes, including subject guides, reference services, event programming, and broadcasting library updates to the public. With Web 2.0 becoming an integral part of library services, libraries are migrating their traditional intranets to Web 2.0 platforms because they facilitate easy creation and harnessing of collective intelligence (de Voil 2008; Kennedy 2007). To guide this transition, practitioners seek out best practices: processes or theoretical models that are believed to lead to the best results. Many libraries have access to traditional intranet best practices, but how well do these best practices translate when applied to an existing Web 2.0 intranet infrastructure?

This case study explores the process of planning, implementing, and evaluating two generations of a Web 2.0 intranet for the technical services department at Miami University of Ohio. Following a brief literature review of intranet best practices is a detailed examination of each stage in the evolution of the departmental intranet: planning, migration/implementation, and the consequences faced with each generation. The discussion section analyzes several aspects of the case study and compares these to the intranet best practices mentioned in the literature review, noting the similarities and differences between the two. The study concludes with a brief discussion of Web 2.0's impact on intranets and speculation on the future of Web 2.0 intranets.

LITERATURE REVIEW

The library literature has seen a rise in case studies dealing with Web 2.0 intranets—wikis, blogs, and so forth—and generally does not compare established best practices from the first generations of intranets to the best practices emerging from Web 2.0 intranets. There has been some documentation of general Web 2.0 intranet best practices outside the library literature under the guise of Enterprise 2.0 (Köhler-Krüner 2009). There are established best practices from various first generation intranets that have been discussed at some length in literature outside of the library field. These best practices cover the planning, implementation, and evaluation cycles in the life of the intranet.

Many of the planning best practices echo key elements found in information architecture. Intranets rely on similar technical infrastructure and tools needed for creating and maintaining Internet pages and applications. The intranet must support many of the same functions as information architecture, including informed decision making, findability of organizational information, information security, content management, and metrics (Kennedy, Littlejohn, and Costanzo 2007). Attentive and thorough planning is required if the intranet is to succeed. Approaches to the adoption of planning best practices vary between loose guiding points to highly structured plans. Certain practitioners have found focusing on a more relaxed planning and management style has led to intranet success (Guenther 2003). This high-level planning touches on broad subjects and issues without systematically determining the planning process, which allows individual organizations greater flexibility in the planning stage. On the other end of the spectrum, other practitioners prefer a more structured approach to planning. For example, some practitioners use enterprise information architecture when planning intranets (Crandall 2007). The more structured enterprise information architecture gives practitioners specific processes and tools that have been tested and tweaked in a variety of situations.

However, not all planning best practices show such a range. Content management planning examples in the literature do not offer the same range in variety as discussed above. An intranet can fail for many reasons; nonetheless, out-of-date, incomplete, or incorrect information on the intranet serves as a major reason for intranet failure (Tredinnick 2004). To avoid failure, the literature generally suggests assigning a manager to be responsible for either personally updating the information or overseeing others who keep the information current (Guenther 2003; Jespersen and Boye 2008; Masrek et al. 2007). In this approach, it is clear who is responsible for content accuracy, and any requests for content updates can be directed to this particular person. This person may also be the intranet manager, since some see the roles of the intranet manager merging with information/document managing responsibilities because of the intranet's dependency on content (White 2008). In any case, the literature suggested that there should be a plan in place to ensure the intranet's content is accurate and current.

Implementation depends on the planning stage and is a major factor in determining the success of the intranet. Practitioners offer a variety of strategies to address implementation issues. Kim Guenther (2003) suggested involving the end users in the intranet development and implementation processes. In this way, end users develop a sense of ownership in the intranet and are more open to integrating the intranet into their daily operations. Others focused on training and setting standards and guidelines for intranet use (Jespersen and Boye 2008). Training allows users not only to understand how the intranet works technically but also gives developers a chance to instruct users about ways the intranet could be used in their daily operations. Taking a more structured approach, Antonella Martini, Mariano Corso, and Luisa Pellegrini (2009) suggested that intranet developers use a formal "change management strategy" to facilitate end-user behavior changes (304). The strategy could help developers in dealing with overall implementation in addition to specific issues that might arise, such as barriers encountered by end users while trying to use the intranet.

While many use planning and implementation best practices as benchmarks for their intranets, evaluation best practices are trickier to tease out from the literature than planning and implementation. Nonetheless, some have covered this area, either by creating hypothetical models or by re-porting what they have used for intranet evaluation at their organization. Mohamad Noorman Masrek et al. (2007) proposed a model that connected intranet effectiveness to a plethora of factors in an organization. These factors correspond with many of the best practices mentioned in previous literature, from upper management's support and end-user ownership to several aspects of content and technology management. Another model, called the intranet efficiency and effectiveness model, focuses more on domains: front end, back end, and people, processes, and technology (Jacoby and Leqi 2007). The front-end domain includes more common information architecture issues, such as accessibility and navigation; the back-end domain deals with search-related issues; and the people, process, and technology domain concerns itself with how the intranet contributes to organizational productivity and supports the requirements assigned by the organization. Again, this model relies on the execution of planning and implementation best practices. Outside of theoretical models, Javier Bargas-Avila et al. (2009) created and tested a questionnaire measuring intranet satisfaction among end-users. The thirteen-item questionnaire measured several facets of content quality and intranet usability. Nonetheless, this survey was limited to measuring satisfaction and did not allow end users the opportunity to provide suggestions and open-ended feedback.

Planning, implementation, and evaluation best practices from first-generation intranets have been tested and modified from a decade of intranet implementations. However, are these best practices transferable to Web 2.0 intranets? The following case study explores the issues demonstrated by an existing Web 2.0 intranet and the actions taken to address these issues.

CASE STUDY: MIAMI UNIVERSITY TECHNICAL SERVICES INTRANET

The Technical Services Department at Miami University comprises several teams: acquisitions, cataloging, database maintenance, authority control, serials and electronic resources, physical processing, and conservation and preservation. Historically, the department employed about five full-time librarians, fifteen full-time paraprofessionals, and a varying number of part-time and visiting librarians, paraprofessionals, and student workers. The department's first intranet was a locally hosted HTML Web site, which was created in 1998 and hosted policies, procedures, and some general staff and department information. The department head and the serials librarian updated the Web site, while the rest of the department had read-only access.

In 2005, the Information Services Department at Miami started to work with MediaWiki (http://www.mediawiki.org; for more information, see

Withers, Bruell, and Casson 2005). An information services librarian involved with the information services wiki discussed the benefits of using MediaWiki as a departmental intranet with several technical services librarians. MediaWiki's editing features offered a way to open the editing process to all departmental staff instead of only the two librarians who had FTP access to update the HTML pages. After some discussion with the information services librarian and other technical services librarians, the Technical Services Department head decided to move the static HTML intranet to a local installation of MediaWiki in late 2005 (see Figure 1) with the hopes that the wiki would alleviate content accuracy issues present in the previous intranet.

When the author joined the Technical Services Department in summer 2008, the wiki intranet had been in production for almost three years. While some of the information was helpful, most was out of date. The wiki, with the exception of additional departmental content, had remained the same since its launch in 2005. There was no evaluation of the wiki during its three years in production. A three-part evaluation of the wiki revealed several major issues in content accuracy, software appropriateness, and integration into the departmental environment.

It was apparent the content on the wiki was not accurate or well maintained. For example, the department moved from Innovative Interfaces' telnet-based integrated library system to the Millenium graphical user interface in 2005. By 2008, only one posted procedure reflected the changeover to the Millennium interface. Staff editing—or lack of editing—played a major factor in the content accuracy issue. Instead of updating the content themselves, many staff went to the secretary to update the wiki. The daunting task of maintaining the growing wiki proved to be even more of a challenge when a new departmental secretary took over the wiki manager role. The new departmental secretary had no experience in markup languages and could regularly update the staff information and the Innovative Interfaces local code pages only with the former secretary's help, which was limited. Content was also hard to find on the wiki. There was no formal navigation structure, so many staff members became frustrated when searching the wiki. They bookmarked wiki pages essential to daily operations and eventually left the rest of the wiki unused.

The staff's hesitancy to edit the wiki themselves led evaluators to examine if MediaWiki was an appropriate fit for the department. MediaWiki had many features that attracted some in the department early on; however, these features did not fit the technical skill set of the majority of the departmental staff. The wiki markup language in MediaWiki proved to be a sticking point for even the experienced staff, although most staff members had experience with a WYSIWG editing environment; MediaWiki's native editing environment was foreign to them. Another indicator that the wiki software was not an appropriate choice for the department was the lack of wiki maintenance. The department was responsible for maintaining the wiki software on the

Technical Services

(Revision as of 22:36, 31 Oct 2009)

 Welcome to Tech Services Wiki

Elizabeth Brice, Department Head

Tech Services Wiki is the place where you'll find staff information, processes and procedures, and resource information. If you'd like to send some feedback about these pages or you find a broken link, please email Debbie Hansel, Department Secretary (a.k.a. The *New* Wiki Woman)

Resources

Bib / Item Codes
Bib / Item Codes for Art and Architecture, Documents, External Collection, IMC, King, Music, Online / Periodicals, Science, Special Collections, and SWORD, ICodes For Statistics, and Status Codes Used in Tech Services For Tracking

Department Information
Department information such as Policies, Fire Exit Plans, Funds Listings, Statistics, and Library Resources (including the *New* list for language skills resources).

Staff Information
Information and resources for Staff. Includes the Staff Directory for Tech Services, the Emergency Telephone Tree, the Travel Form required to be completed by Unclassified Staff, Training and Information for New Employees, and Work Schedules.

Teams
A list of each team for easy access to the team's roster, mission statement, policies, procedures, and documentation.

Projects and Current Status Report

Wiki Re-organization
Project Name

TS Announcements

New! Healthy Habits Team!

Mission Statement

"To acquire, organize, preserve, and disseminate information resources in support of the mission and purposes of Miami University Libraries with an emphasis on quality, timeliness, accountability, and pride."

People of Tech Services

FIGURE 1 MediaWiki version of Technical Service Intranet.

local server. No one was assigned to maintain the wiki software, leading to missed upgrades and the lack of integration of MediaWiki extensions.

An informal online survey of the departmental environment was conducted to determine how the wiki factored into the departmental environment. Staff anonymously answered questions regarding wiki use and their opinions about the current wiki. Half of the department responded to the survey. The survey showed that while the staff used select parts of the wiki, like the library location codes page, the staff felt either indifferent or uncomfortable with using the wiki as a whole. The majority seldom or never edited the wiki because it felt uncomfortable or did not know how to edit the wiki. As previously mentioned, the staff bookmarked wiki pages they used on a daily basis and went beyond the wiki to obtain and document information. In summary, the wiki intranet was not integrated into the department.

After surveying the three areas of content, software appropriateness, and departmental integration, the evaluation of the MediaWiki intranet illustrated the wiki intranet did not live up to its goal of creating greater access to departmental information. Department staff could not maintain the software; the wiki also presented new issues with software maintenance and content policies. The challenge facing the department was to reinvent the intranet to reach its full potential while avoiding the above issues.

PLANNING THE SECOND-GENERATION WEB 2.0 DEPARTMENTAL INTRANET

In light of the evaluation of the first wiki intranet, the mission of the second-generation wiki intranet focused on content revitalization, modifying wiki navigation structures, and further customizing MediaWiki with several extensions that would add usability and function lacking from the current installation. In the early planning stages, the decision was made to involve as many departmental staff members as possible to allow staff to tailor the intranet to meet their needs. To facilitate discussion and ideas with the department, a wiki reorganization page was created in the wiki, explaining the mission, stages, and beta versions of updated wiki pages or procedures (see Figure 2). In addition, volunteers were requested when the reorganization project was announced.

Staff members were most heavily involved in content planning. Each team in the department had a point person responsible for guiding the process of either updating or creating policies and procedures for his team. While teams focused on their procedures, others dealt with updating, archiving, or deleting pages that included one of the more than 90 broad types of information on the wiki. Staff reviewed the content based on potential impact on departmental workflow, currency, and importance. From this review, a core of content categories—training, macro files, team information, procedures/policies, staff information, resources and tools, and statistics—rose from the updating and weeding of the MediaWiki content. These categories

Wiki Re-organization

From Technical Services Wiki

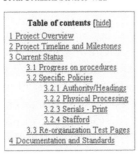
[edit]

Project Overview

Primary Contact: Becky Yoose

This is the project page for the updating and re-organization of the TS wiki. The project benchmarks are set below, but there is some wiggle room for submitting updated procedures, since I will be doing a lot of formatting and revisions during November.

Project Timeline and Milestones

[edit]

- **September - October 2008**: Collect updated procedures, send back revisions
- **November 2008**: Start publishing revised procedures, navigation, archiving old procedures
- **End of December 2008**: Finish!

Current Status

[edit]

Address to new wiki - http://tsmuohio.pbwiki.com

Progress on procedures

[edit]

Dept/Procedure	Status
Authority/Headings	Revisions completed, ready to post
CC	Revisions completed, ready to post
Ordering	Waiting for first draft
Physical Processing	Revisions completed, ready to post
Receipt	First Draft - revising
Serials - Print	First Draft - revising
Serials - Electronic	Waiting for first draft
Stafford Project	First Draft - revising

Specific Policies

[edit]
[edit]

Authority/Headings

- Authority Control
- Weekly Headings List
- OCLC Holdings Update

FIGURE 2 Wiki Re-organization project page.

became the wiki's main navigational structure. To facilitate findability, the wiki's organizational structure was broad and shallow, reducing the maximum number of clicks to a specific page to three.

To improve the usability of the wiki intranet, the initial plan was to take advantage of the various MediaWiki's extensions, including the WYSIWIG FCKeditor plug-in and to use the customizable side navigation menu. However, the plug-in required a certain version of MediaWiki. The local installation of MediaWiki was years behind the latest version, and upgrading the wiki meant either doing a clean install of the latest version or performing numerous incremental upgrades. To add to the software troubles, the author (with admin status) could not perform several admin functions, such as editing the side bar navigation menu. The other wiki administrators encountered the same problem, which persisted even after referring to MediaWiki documentation and troubleshooting materials. This made the plan to improve wiki navigation much more difficult.

The wiki installation presented major problems that needed careful consideration. If the department continued to use the existing installation, then the department faced numerous updates in a short period, with each upgrade bringing risks such as disappearing content, broken functions, or other version issues. On the other hand, the upgrades could have restored admin privileges and allowed for wider extension use. The problems also forced the reconsideration of software maintenance plans. While the author originally planned to take on the majority of software maintenance duties, the question remained as to who would take over maintenance when the author moved on to a new set of job responsibilities. The author considered the tradeoffs of installing the newer version as well as other options before deciding which action to take. In the end, it was decided that moving away from MediaWiki would be the best option.

Several alternatives to MediaWiki were reviewed. At the time, several librarians and staff members were working with Drupal (http://drupal.org/), a content management system, in building a next-generation online public access catalog (OPAC). One of the lead developers of the new OPAC advised that Drupal might not be the best option because his previous experiences using Drupal as a wiki echoed concerns about the software maintenance. The developer suggested the department look into hosted options. The developer specifically suggested PBWiki (now PBWorks, http://pbworks.com/). PBWiki's software maintenance was the responsibility of the hosting company, who would be in charge of upgrades and other software maintenance. PBWiki's free academic version offered password protection, online document management tools, and a WYSIWYG editor that mimicked an editing environment with which staff were familiar.

A PBWiki intranet mockup was created that contained a few updated procedures, brief staff and department information, and a few new items, such as an embedded staff calendar using Google Calendar, for the department head. While the mockup looked promising, the department head needed to ensure that staff would be receptive to the new software. The mockup intranet was then sent to the point people in each departmental team and asked for feedback. Reactions were positive overall. The WYSI-WIG editing received the most praise, with the right-side navigation menus receiving positive comments as well. After studying the feedback from staff, the department head decided that PBWiki would suit the department better than MediaWiki.

IMPLEMENTING THE SECOND-GENERATION WEB 2.0 DEPARTMENTAL INTRANET

After the decision to go with PBWiki, work began on fleshing out the proof of concept. The navigation used the categories developed from the content planning. The main sidebar listed all the categories, while the document management sidebar provided access to macro files. As soon as the majority of updated material was migrated to PBWiki, a month-long beta-testing period began, with the point people for content updating serving as beta testers. Through their help in updating core content, testing, and suggestions, the new wiki intranet launched to the entire department in January 2009 (see Figure 3).

The launch coincided with a required hands-on training session for all staff members. The training covered wiki search and navigation, uploading files, and creating and editing individuals' staff pages. To supplement the training courses, one-on-one training sessions were offered and wiki training materials were created.

Generally, departmental staff reacted positively to the new wiki. Like the beta testers, the staff members praised the WYSIWYG editor and easy navigation. The staff appreciated having easily accessible, easily editable current content. Nonetheless, the staff had some concerns as well. The requirement of creating a PBWiki account to access the wiki meant they had to keep track of yet another login. Several staff members had their passwords reset multiple times during the first few months after implementation. Nonetheless, the staff welcomed the intranet change.

DISCUSSION

The case study shows that Web 2.0 intranets face similar challenges to traditional intranets. Because of this similarity in issues, Web 2.0 intranets benefit from some of the same best practices established for traditional intranets, especially in the planning stage. Implementation and evaluation practices are similar for both traditional and Web 2.0 intranets, but Web 2.0 intranets have their own unique issues that need to be addressed.

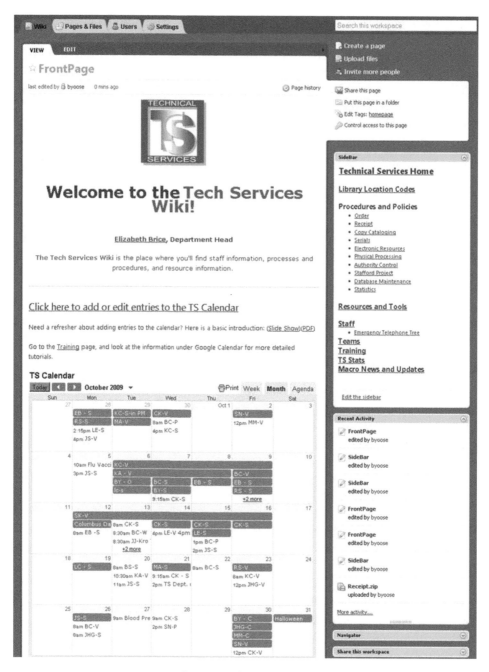

FIGURE 3 PBWiki version for Technical Services Intranet.

Planning

Detailed and structured planning worked very well, especially in technology choices and content management. Researching various technologies and intranet setups during the planning process played a key role in the successful planning of the PBWiki intranet. The department did not have the resources to maintain the MediaWiki local installation, nor did the majority of the staff feel confident in using a wiki markup language. PBWiki, on the other hand, fit better in regards to resources for maintenance and staff skills. It was critical to ensure the physical intranet setup matched the skill set of the majority of staff in the organization as well as the available resources that the organization can contribute to the maintenance of the intranet.

Content management planning combined with elements of information architecture also proved to be vital in the planning stages. Critical information, including policies and procedures, were updated and migrated while other information was archived. A navigation plan sorted and categorized where certain types of information would live on the intranet and provided multiple points of access for browsing and searching. Trimming down the MediaWiki intranet content during the migration helped make PBWiki more focused in navigational structure and allowed easier access.

Communication between staff involved with intranet planning and other departmental staff during planning was another critical area for the intranet's success. By creating opportunities for staff to participate in the development process and encouraging such participation, the planners of the PBWiki intranet helped cultivate a sense of shared intranet ownership. The more involved the department became, the more the intranet became the department's intranet—built, owned, and maintained by the staff as a whole—instead of being another departmental intranet that was the responsibility of a few.

Implementation

Beta testing before the PBWiki intranet's release to the department not only addressed the intranet's bugs but also allowed for vital feedback on navigation and intranet functionality. The feedback during the beta period helped ensure the intranet focused on what the staff needed—documentation, easy access to information, etc.—and ways to better organize the intranet content to facilitate access and usability. The emphasis on training from the beginning of the implementation stage to the present gave the staff much needed guidance in switching intranet applications and helping them to build a skill baseline where they could competently perform basic tasks such as editing.

It would be incorrect to say, however, that implementing a departmental Web 2.0 intranet does not have its own challenges. The greatest challenge faced in the case study stemmed from a feature that is a cornerstone to Web 2.0 applications and philosophy. The ability to easily edit and share information with Web 2.0 is one of its main selling points; however, these features could also cause the intranet to fail. Although the department had a wiki manager who was responsible for the overall well-being of the

MediaWiki intranet, staff members were expected to edit the wiki when they saw fit. However, a mismatch between technology and staff skills plus existing organizational habits incurred from the first intranet contributed to the decay of the first wiki intranet. It was very easy to assume the technology would do the heavy lifting of changing people's information sharing behavior; however, implementing a Web 2.0 intranet requires greater diligence by the implementers to avoid falling into a false sense of security and requires a greater emphasis on staff buy-in and integration into daily operations.

Evaluation

Evaluation relied mostly on benchmarks from planning and implementation best practices. It was not hard to conclude that the MediaWiki intranet failed, since many benchmarks from planning and implementation best practices (content currency, technology maintenance plan, baseline skills present in majority of staff, etc.) were not met. A survey was also used in the evaluation process; however, unlike the survey mentioned in the literature review, this survey focused on qualitative data, with the majority of questions being open ended. This survey could be seen as the first step in initiating communication for the reorganization/migration project. While none of the theoretical models mentioned in the brief literature review at the time of the MediaWiki evaluation was used, the models could have retrospectively aided in the evaluation process.

Evaluation of the Web 2.0 intranet depended on the application used and the roles and mission given to the intranet. The first Web 2.0 intranet was a wiki; therefore, there were certain unspoken expectations that came with that specific application, such as the staff editing the wiki, as mentioned above. Traditional intranet evaluation best practices gave some guidance. The evaluation of the first wiki intranet focused on content and software management issues and on general staff opinions. Guidelines for Web 2.0 intranet evaluation beyond benchmarking, planning, and implementing best practices are still undefined. What is the threshold for the number of staff edits to determine an intranet wiki's success? Does this threshold change with different types of information housed in the intranet? It may be that general Web 2.0 intranet evaluation guidelines may not be appropriate, since each Web 2.0 application is unique unto itself.

CONCLUSION

Intranets are a product of the need for organizing and creating access to organizational knowledge to all members in an organization. This need also embodies a desire to create a tool to foster collaboration and collective knowledge building not only to increase the knowledge captured by the intranet but also to increase the quality of knowledge captured and the quality of work done in the organization. The first generation of intranets created access to information but did not have the ability to incorporate collaboration. Web 2.0 applications give intranets the chance to fulfill the desire for collaboration. Since libraries themselves thrive on information sharing and collaboration, Web 2.0 applications seem the logical choice for an intranet. Library practitioners need to keep in mind that the intranet, whether traditional or Web 2.0-based, should not be approached lightly. As explored above, several best practices for traditional intranets helped with the successful launch of the current departmental Web 2.0 intranet:

- constant communication between intranet developers and end users,
- involving end users in planning process,
- content management,
- beta testing,
- training emphasis before/at implementation, and
- evaluation based on staff feedback and interaction with intranet.

Web 2.0 intranets do benefit from these practices. What is more specifically needed, however, is more information to determine Web 2.0 intranet specific best practices:

- the process of choosing a particular type of Web 2.0 application for an intranet;
- evaluation of Web 2.0 intranets, both specific to the application and in general;
- cultivating the Web 2.0 philosophy of sharing and active participation within an organization before, during, and after implementation of a Web 2.0 intranet; and
- migration from a traditional to a Web 2.0 intranet or from one Web 2.0 application to another.

While the case study above touches on some of the above points, it covers only one organization and one Web 2.0 application type. Establishing these best practices for Web 2.0 intranets will help the first wave of first-generation Web 2.0 intranets and beyond succeed.

ACKNOWLEDGMENTS

The author would like to thank Elizabeth Brice, head of Technical Services and assistant dean, and Carol Klumb, program associate, for their assistance in the section describing the history of the departmental intranet up to 2008.

The author would also like to thank Jody Perkins, metadata librarian, for providing feedback and suggestions during the preparation of the manuscript.

REFERENCES

Bargas-Avila, Javier, Jonas Lötscher, Sébastien Orsini, and Klaus Opwis. 2009. Intranet satisfaction questionnaire: Development and validation of a questionnaire to measure user satisfaction with the intranet. *Computers in Human Behavior* 25(6): 1241–1250.

Crandall, Mike. 2007. Information architecture. In *Intranets for info pros*, eds. Mary Lee Kennedy and Jane Dysart, 183–205. Medford, NJ: Information Today.

de Voil, Nick. 2008. Web 2.0's effects on intranet usability—and why it matters. *Cutter IT Journal* 21(8): 12–16.

Guenther, Kim. 2003. Ten steps to intranet success. *Online* 27(1): 66–69.

Jacoby, Grant A., and Luqi. 2007. Intranet model and metrics: Measuring intranet overall value contributions based on a corporation's critical business requirements. *Communications of the ACM* 50(2): 43–50.

Jespersen, Dorthe R., and Janus Boye. 2008. Untangling enterprise wikis. *EContent* 31(9): 30–34.

Kennedy, Mary Lee. 2007. Introduction. In *Intranets for info pros*, eds. Mary Lee Kennedy and Jane Dysart, 1–13. Medford, NJ: Information Today.

Kennedy, Mary Lee, Ian Littlejohn, and Cory Costanzo. 2007. Current state considerations and future direction of intranets. In *Intranets for info pros*, eds. Mary Lee Kennedy and Jane Dysart, 15–30. Medford, New Jersey: Information Today.

Köhler-Krüner, Hans. 2009. Best practices for implementing enterprise 2.0. *Infonomics* 23(4): 40–45.

Martini, Antonella, Mariano Corso, and Luisa Pellegrini. 2009. An empirical roadmap for intranet evolution. *International Journal of Information Management* 29: 295–308.

Masrek, Mohamad Noorman, Nor Shahriza, Abdul Karim, and Ramlah Hussein. 2007. Investigating corporate intranet effectiveness: A conceptual framework. *Information Management & Computer Security* 15(3): 168–183.

Tredinnick Luke. 2004. *Why intranets fail (and how to fix them): A practical guide for information professionals*. Oxford, England: Chandos.

White, Martin. 2008. New roles for Intranet managers. *EContent* 31(8): 24.

Withers, Robert, Kris Bruell, and Rob Casson. 2005. Something wiki this way comes: An interactive way of posting, updating, and tracking changes in information used by library staff. *College & Research Libraries News* 66(11): 775–777.

Who Moved My Intranet? The Human Side of Introducing Collaborative Technologies to Library Staff

KEVEN JEFFERY

Library & Information Access, San Diego State University, San Diego, California, USA

ELLIE DWORAK

Albertsons Library, Boise State University, Boise, Idaho, USA

Intranets can be crucial tools in fostering communication within an academic library. This article describes the successful implementation of an intranet wiki at the San Diego State University Library & Information Access. The steps involved with implementing, marketing, and supporting the MediaWiki software are described, and the results of a user survey are discussed. The survey, which was answered by 50 percent of intranet users, indicated that while the intranet was well used by all respondents, librarians were more active and more comfortable using the editing features of the wiki software. Recommendations for similar projects are offered based on the findings and experiences.

INTRODUCTION

In fall 2007, the San Diego State University (SDSU) Library migrated from a static HTML intranet to a wiki intranet using MediaWiki (Wikimedia Foundation) software (http://www.mediawiki.org). The MediaWiki software was chosen because it was open source, used software (PHP and MySQL) supported at the library and had a large user community, including the popular Wikipedia free encyclopedia (http://wikipedia.org). This migration was completed by two librarians and an IT staff person, who was also the intranet Webmaster. In doing so, the group shifted the responsibility for content development and maintenance from a single Webmaster (with several backups) to all library employees. This change was made in the hopes that this would lead to a more dynamic, relevant, and current intranet. For such a major reallocation of accountability to be successful, library employees had to be persuaded to participate in this process. Without voluntarily participation, the move to this new, more dynamic format would be a wasted effort. This article explores the measures that were taken to garner involvement in this technology change, analyzes the results of these efforts, and offers suggestions and next steps.

LITERATURE REVIEW

According to Hamilton Mphidi and Retha Snyman (2004), intranets can, among other things, be used to share knowledge, create trust, and improve decision making and services (394). They are, therefore, an important addition to the communication tools of any large organization, including libraries. The development of a successful intranet has been compared to an evolutionary process that occurs over time and involves a range of actors within an organization (Martini, Corso, and Pellegrini 2009, 295–296). It is consequently important in the success of an intranet to create value for both the organization and the employees who will rely on it as a communication tool. A key part of this process is to involve everyone in the project (301).

Evaluations of library intranets, however, have found that librarians and professionals can be more invested in online communication than supporting staff members, who can be unaware of the tool or believe it is not targeted to them (Robbins, Engel, and Bierman 2006, 270). While it is no doubt important to have top-level encouragement for Web 2.0 adoption (Köhler-Krüner 2009, 42–43), it is perhaps more important that staff members are completely involved. Staff should be fully invested, not only as an exercise in morale building, but also because many students have been found to not differentiate between the types of academic library employees assisting them. These students expect all library employees to have the tools to answer their questions in a satisfactory manner (Sult and Evangeliste 2009, 249–250). If staff members are left out of the information-sharing process, library patrons are in danger of not receiving a consistently high level of service.

Creating online collaboration and information sharing between organizational actors is a strength of wiki software. Wikis can be used as storehouses of institutional knowledge, aiding reference desk staff (Dworak and Jeffery 2009, 404), and can, perhaps more importantly, become a "collective resource" helping to remind each employee that they are responsible for intranet content (409). Wikis, like any Web 2.0 tool, are also useful, as they democratize access to the method of creating content, avoiding the danger that information technology staff members are the only drivers of software adoption (Köhler-Krüner 2009, 42).

Intranets can be unsuccessful for a multitude of reasons, including the failure to consider the organizational goals, lack of vision, absence of commitment and responsibility, conflicts, and role misunderstandings (Martini et al. 2009, 296). It seems that the collaborative nature of the wiki can overcome many of these issues, especially in an organization where there is a continuous drive for improvement (Köhler-Krüner 2009, 42).

CULTIVATING INCLUSION

The SDSU Library is a fairly large organization, with 28 librarians, 53 staff members, and four administrators. There are only one or two layers of management between front-line employees and the dean of the library. While technology change always requires a level of staff buy-in, it is crucial in an organization where individuals are given a great deal of responsibility for determining how they do their daily work, as is the case in a flatly structured organization.

The methods this group used to build staff involvement required effort in the areas of communication and training. Anecdotally, the major reasons for technology adoption failures at the SDSU Library were that users did not know who to talk to or that the service was available, users were intimidated by the change, or users felt too busy to dedicate time to learning something new. By offering training and support, the implementation group tried to alleviate the concerns about the wiki being too complicated or otherwise intimidating, offer employees a dedicated time to learn the new tool, and continuously market the new software.

Recognizing the importance of buy-in, the intranet team encouraged involvement by conducting surveys, transferring content, conducting workshops, and recruiting wiki administrators. The team communicated with library staff by conducting pre- and post-surveys, transferring the old intranet content from HTML to wiki markup, conducting several hands-on wiki editing workshops, recruiting several wiki administrators to serve as departmental experts, and updating and questioning staff via e-mail and in-person communications. Each of these is addressed below.

The main purpose of the pre-survey was to gain an understanding of how the current HTML-based intranet was being used and what could be improved. The focus of the post-survey was to determine the success of the wiki transfer and to discover any needs for follow-up. However, both had the hidden benefit of reminding people that an intranet is not a static apparatus imposed upon them by the IT department but a shared tool meant to be used and useful. It also indicated to library employees that the team cared about their opinions and were considering them while developing a project plan. This is vital because without trust, the chances of gaining acceptance for a major change are slim.

Once the pre-survey was complete and a wiki was chosen as the best solution, the content transfer was done almost exclusively by the project group. While such an action may appear to decrease involvement, presenting a ready-to-use product made the transition easier and encouraged future involvement by removing a large, time-intensive block of work. Library personnel understandably react more positively to being told they are being helped to do creative work than simply being asked to add something new to their workload.

Arguably the most important action in increasing comfort with the new Internet was a series of wiki-editing workshops held by the project group. These workshops were scheduled strategically so the staff had a choice of the most convenient time. During training, attendees were issued logins and passwords, which they could use to edit the wiki. Handouts were given outlining the basics of wiki markup and library Web procedures. After a brief introduction, the majority of the hour-long session was spent adding and editing content in the wiki. This allowed some staff to get comfortable enough to accept the project right away, while others felt the need for more help. Individuals were encouraged to come to multiple workshops, and one-on-one help was offered to those who requested it.

After each workshop, attendees were asked if they would like to be given administrative rights to the wiki. Administrative rights allow users to create and erase pages and assign user names and passwords. Users who do not have administrative privileges can only edit existing pages. The goal here was to have at least one wiki administrator per library department. This goal was easily met; in fact, many departments had more than one administrator. This created a support system for those who forgot information, needed help, or were new to the library. It also initiated a group of advocates who were excited about the project.

Throughout this process, many e-mails were sent to update library staff on the progress of the project, next steps, and workshop opportunities. Through both e-mail and verbal invitations during workshops, questions and comments were encouraged and help was offered for any wiki issues. Quite a few people took advantage of these opportunities and offered their feedback, asked for help, or both. In fact, other wiki administrators were recruited via these communications.

The ability to build involvement was enhanced by several factors. First, one section of the intranet is the heavily used and often updated "Ready Reference File." This knowledge base comprises the shared institutional experience of the reference staff and includes information such as "how to find resources for that difficult English 476 assignment" and "how to locate theses and dissertations in the online catalog." As with the rest of the intranet, prior to implementation of the wiki, changes to the Ready Reference File had to be made by sending requests to one of the several people with the ability to make changes to the HTML documents. Unlike some other parts of the intranet, the Ready Reference File requires continuous updating, since assignments, item locations, and other information changes frequently. Further, out-of-date content was often noticed immediately because of the public service nature of the subject matter. Employees who worked at the reference desk saw immediate value in being able to update the Ready Reference File on their own, and the project gained traction fairly quickly within this department.

Another advantage was that, at this time, the library was undergoing a round of strategic planning, and several strategic planning groups were distributing frequent status updates and draft reports among the library staff. The wiki was an excellent place to post such documents. Unlike with e-mail, people were not being inundated with draft after draft of planning group reports but instead could find the latest version on the wiki at their convenience. The MediaWiki software used for the project includes automatic version tracking so people could see what had changed or revert to an earlier version in the event of an error.

Finally, several library employees felt the wiki had great potential value and championed the project from the start, both by posting materials and encouraging others to do so. While one of these people was an administrator, it was more a matter of cultural adjustment than a top-down impetus that caused the new model to take hold. Because several people were posting materials to the wiki and directing others to read them there, it became an obvious option for the distribution of materials.

Despite the significant efforts put into training and communication, there was still room for improvement. Rather than giving user-level passwords only to people who attended a workshop, everybody in the library should have been issued a password. This would have allowed people to practice and experiment with the wiki software prior to making a decision about attending a workshop; in fact, it may have encouraged them to come. Still others may not have needed to attend a workshop, given that the software is fairly intuitive. It also would have been a good idea to hold workshops after the project rollout rather than considering them exclusively a pre-launch portion of the project.

SURVEY RESULTS

The project team has conducted three surveys during the course of this project. The first two, mentioned earlier, were carried out directly before and after the implementation. The first, a pre-survey, was used to gauge the need for the change as well as to determine direction, while the second, a post-survey, was used to assess success. More discussion of these surveys can be found in a 2009 article by Ellie Dworak and Keven Jeffery. Full results data are available from the authors.

A follow-up survey (see Appendix A) was sent about one year after the post-survey and two years after the wiki implementation; the intent of this final survey was to measure the success of integrating the shift from centralized to distributed intranet management and to determine whether there was a need for related efforts. This survey differed considerably from the first two surveys, as it sought information about training needs and integration issues rather than trying to ascertain a need for a new software product or to determine its technical success. As a side note, these surveys were not conducted as statistical studies but as tools to guide and direct the project.

The recent follow-up survey found that of the 40 survey respondents, 98 percent had used the wiki to look up information at least once over the past six months, and 78 percent had reported using it at least once a week. In comparison, 53 percent of survey respondents used the intranet at least once a week prior to the wiki implementation, and 64 percent used it directly post-implementation (Dworak and Jeffery 2009, 407). This upward trend suggests that the wiki has become an increasingly valuable information source for the librarians and staff.

As might be imagined, there were far fewer wiki editors than wiki readers; only half the follow-up survey respondents (48 percent) reported making a change to the wiki themselves. The types of information users reported updating most often were the reference department Ready Reference File (28 percent), committee information (23 percent), department information (23 percent), and information related to a recent library strategic planning initiative (26 percent). This shows a noticeable increase in changes initiated by staff over our previous surveys. Before the wiki project, only 28 percent of survey respondents had made a change to the intranet by any means, including asking the Webmaster to make a change. In the second, post-wiki survey, this number jumped to 40 percent (Dworak and Jeffery 2009, 407).

The 50 percent of respondents who did not report making a change to the wiki themselves also did not contact wiki administrators to make changes for them. These individuals did, however, report using the wiki content, as 95 percent had visited the wiki over the past six months and 65 percent visited it at least once a week. Seventy percent of the individuals who chose not to update content were staff members, not librarians, and only 30 percent of these non-editors had received any training using the wiki software. It was interesting to note, however, that 45 percent of these non-editors were interested in receiving more wiki training, suggesting that there is an opportunity to involve some of them in the content management process.

Acceptance of the wiki as a communication tool seems to be largely spearheaded by librarians. Eighty-three percent of the seventeen librarian respondents reported using the wiki at least once a week, and 65 percent reported changing wiki content themselves. This can be compared to the 22 library staff respondents, of whom 73 percent reported visiting the wiki at least once a week, with only 32 percent making a change to the wiki themselves. Furthermore, while 50 percent of librarians reported they were more likely to update content because of the wiki, only 27 percent of support staff reported a similar feeling.

At the SDSU Library, the responsibility for updating online content is largely shared by librarians and staff. The different rates of acceptance by librarians and support staff might be explained by the greater success in marketing training sessions to librarians during the launch of the wiki. Sixty percent of librarian respondents reported having received wiki training either in a workshop or individually, while only 41 percent of staff reported the same. There was also a significant difference between librarians and staff members regarding the perception of the wiki being easy to use on their own. Forty-one percent of librarian respondents stated the wiki was easy to use without help, while only 14 percent of staff had a similar feeling. This survey did not investigate why this might be, but librarians do have expertise in navigating interfaces and may not find the wiki software to be any more difficult than using complex research databases.

The difference between librarian and staff adoption might also be explained by librarians having a more immediate need to share information, as with the Ready Reference File. However, the latest survey suggests the library could do a better job of marketing the wiki and providing wiki training to library support staff. Perhaps part of this process could involve encouraging the posting of materials to the wiki that would be of more interest to staff members, such as department manuals and training material.

CONCLUSION

New technology implementations fail for many reasons, the most critical being a situation where there is no significant need for the new technology. When trying to develop projects that benefit from distributed input, it is important that project initiators not get caught up in the trendiness of a technology or that they themselves would like to use it or forget to analyze the real benefits and goals of their mission. This is easy to do, because often the people implementing such a project are engaged with and enjoy using new technologies.

Once a real need has been determined, it is important to time a project so that it is not competing with other big technology projects. However, there are always other things going on in a library, so perfect timing may not be achievable. Instead of looking for the ideal time, determine how the change or new tool can support any ongoing or short-term work. The strategic planning process described above benefitted from the wiki, which helped facilitate the adoption and acceptance process. If such convergences are identified, forge contacts with the leaders of those efforts and see if they are willing to promote the project.

A perceived need can be just as important as a real need. A new technology may indeed improve processes or outcomes, but if people do not realize this, they will not feel a need to engage. For this purpose, words are not as effective as experience. Thus, providing time for people to try a new product is crucial, as is following up with refreshers and opportunities for those who were not early adopters but have heard how great the new tool is. The hands-on nature of these sessions cannot be stressed enough, since it is by actually using the new technology that users may begin to understand its utility. Ideally, workshops would be followed with real use, such as at SDSU, where employees posted strategic planning documents and made changes to the Ready Reference File. This will reinforce the learning that takes place in a classroom and encourages the new direction.

While technical skills are highly valued in libraries, the person doing the back-end work does not always have time to manage the training and ongoing communication needed for a successful project. It is important to pull together an implementation team that includes somebody who can serve as a main point of contact for questions and concerns, arrange and market training sessions, and identify the need for further training as the project continues. Too many projects become orphaned after an initial push because this final step is ignored.

Finally, throughout a new technology rollout, attention should be given to those who champion the project. These people may work at any level of the library, from management to student employees. They are the ones whose eyes light up when they are offered a workshop, who ask questions, and who seek opportunities to use the tool. Seek opportunities to send these people out as evangelists and assistants; often, they are happy to be asked.

There are many factors in the success of integrating and accepting a new technology in a library. The most important is connecting the technology to real or perceived needs. Also crucial are plentiful training opportunities, favorable circumstances, and the nurturing of early adopters. If attention is given to all of these areas, a technology project is much more likely to succeed.

REFERENCES

Dworak, Ellie, and Keven Jeffery. 2009. Wiki to the rescue: Creating a more dynamic intranet. *Library Hi Tech* 27(3): 403–410.

Köhler-Krüner, Hanns. 2009. Best practices for implementing enterprise 2.0. *Infonomics* 23(4): 40–45.

Martini, Antonella, Mariano Corso, and Luisa Pellegrini. 2009. An empirical roadmap for intranet evolution. *International Journal of Information Management* 29(4): 295–308.

Mphidi, Hamilton, and Retha Snyman. 2004. The utilisation of an intranet as a knowledge management tool in academic libraries. *The Electronic Library* 22(5): 393–400.

Robbins, Sarah, Debra Engel, and James Bierman. 2006. Using the library intranet to manage Web content. *Library Hi Tech* 24(2): 261–272.

Sult, Leslie, and Mary Evangeliste. 2009. We are all librarians: Training in the ever evolving information commons. *The Reference Librarian* 50(3): 248–258.

APPENDIX A: SDSU LIBRARY AND INFORMATION ACCESS

Wiki Follow-Up Survey

1. What is your role in the library?
   (Answers: Librarian, Staff, Administrator, Student Assistant, not applicable, other (please specify))

2. What department do you work in (check all that apply)?
   (Answers: Acquisitions, Administrative Office, Cataloging (monographs or serials), Circulation, Collection Development, Copy Services, Current Periodicals & Microforms Center, Government Publications, Interlibrary Loan, Information and Digital Technologies, Library Instruction, Media Center, Reference Services, Reserve Book Room, Special Collections & University Archives, Student Computing Center, not applicable, other (please specify))

3. How many times in the past six months have you looked for information on LfolksWiki?
   (Answers: every day, once a week, once a month, once or twice in the last 6 months, not at all)

4. How many times in the past six months have you initiated a change to information contained on the LfolksWiki by contacting the Wiki administrator?
   (Answers: never, 1 time, 2–5 times, 6–10 times, more than 10 times, not applicable)

5. How many times in the past six months have you initiated a change to information contained on the LfolksWiki by posting the information yourself?
   (Answers: never, 1 time, 2–5 times, 6–10 times, more than 10 times, not applicable)

6. What type of information have you updated on the LfolksWiki?
   (Answers: The Ready Reference File; Committee Information; Department Information; Strategic Planning Information; procedures, manuals,

or instructions for library activities; I have not updated any information; other (please specify))

7. If you don't use the Wiki, what's stopping you?
   (Answers: I don't have information to share, I don't have a password, I've forgotten my password, I'm not comfortable with the software, it's easier to get someone to post for me, I do use the wiki, other (please specify))

8. Have you received training on the Wiki software?
   (Answers: yes, I went to a Wiki training session; yes, I received one-on-one instruction from a Wiki administrator; yes, I was shown by a colleague; no, I learned to use the Wiki on my own; no, but I don't use the wiki at all)

9. Would you like to see the library have more training sessions?
   (Answers: yes, more training sessions would be good; no, having the Wiki administrators to ask questions of is enough; no, the Wiki is easy enough to use without training; no, I'm not interested in using the Wiki)

10. Due to the Wiki software you are:
    (Answers: more likely to initiate a change to the Lfolks Web site, just as likely or unlikely to initiate a change to the Lfolks Web site, less likely to initiate a change to the Lfolks Web site)

11. Do you have any comments about this survey or the LfolksWiki Web site that you'd like to share?

Organizational and Social Factors in the Adoption of Intranet 2.0: A Case Study

BOHYUN KIM

Florida International University Medical Library, Miami, Florida, USA

This article presents a case study of the intranet implementation and adoption process of a SharePoint intranet at a small academic library and investigates why the many Web 2.0 tools of the library intranet are currently underused. Staff interviews showed that common goals for an intranet, such as information dissemination, knowledge sharing, communication, and collaboration, are not necessarily easier to achieve when an intranet is equipped with Web 2.0 functionalities. The same level of thorough planning and organizational efforts required to make an intranet succeed before Web 2.0 is still necessary to realize the promise of Intranet 2.0.

Before Intranet 2.0, early intranets attempted to improve organizational performance by facilitating communication and information and knowledge sharing inside an organization. They consisted of static Web pages inside a firewall that only employees could access and view, and their content was centrally collected and distributed. Early intranets functioned primarily as unidirectional communication channels that carried messages and announcements from management to employees.

Intranet 2.0 has the potential to transform an intranet into a dynamic platform for collaboration. By providing Web 2.0 tools, Intranet 2.0 allows employees to freely interact with their colleagues and to publish their own content without relying on an intranet administrator. The use of collaborative technologies in intranets has been shown to have a positive effect on an organization's performance (Merono-Cerdan, Soto-Acosta, and Lopez-Nicolas 2008). However, according to the recent Intranet 2.0 Global Survey (Mills 2010), the rate of satisfaction with Web 2.0 tools in intranets is low. Only 29 percent of organizations rated Intranet 2.0 tool functionality as good or very good. Almost as many organizations (24 percent) rated Intranet 2.0 tool functionality as poor or very poor.

Many organizations see intranet implementation as a purely techno-logical project, but this approach has serious drawbacks. The adoption of Web 2.0 tools only partially depends on their technical capabilities; many organizational and social factors can hinder employees' adoption of Intranet 2.0. Most of all, the purely technological approach overlooks the fundamen-tally social nature of Web 2.0 tools, which require the right environment to thrive.

Using a case study of the Florida International University (FIU) Medical Library SharePoint intranet, this article investigates why many Web 2.0 tools in an intranet are often underused and explores how organizational and social factors play a key role in employees' adoption of Intranet 2.0. In this article, the term, Web 2.0, is applied not only to the typical Web 2.0 tools, such as blogs and wikis, but also to other intranet tools that provide users with the read/write access to create and publish content, such as the link, calendar, announcement, discussion forum, and task tools. The application of the term Web 2.0 to these tools is consistent with the user-driven nature of Web 2.0.

WHAT IS INTRANET 2.0?

Intranet 2.0 is a term used to describe the changes Web 2.0 tools brought to intranets. While "Enterprise 2.0" is also often used almost interchangeably, Enterprise 2.0 includes the use of Web 2.0 tools not only within organizations but also between companies and their partners or customers (McAfee 2006). Web 2.0 is a concept that is notoriously difficult to define. Tim O'Reilly (2005), who popularized this term, clarified its meaning by pointing out the principal features of Web 2.0, which include "control over unique and hard-to-recreate data sources that get richer as more people use them, trusting users as co-developers, and harnessing collective intelligence" (n.p.). These principal features cited make it clear that the defining characteristic of Web 2.0 is "user-driven." Emphasizing this point, David D. Oberhelman (2007, 5) also noted that Web 2.0 creates a distributed form of authority in which the boundaries between site creator and visitor are blurred. Intranet 2.0 empowers users with Web 2.0 tools. Users may directly contribute content to or interact, communicate, or collaborate with their colleagues without the mediation of an intranet administrator.

The prevalence of Web 2.0 tools brought the importance of user participation and interactivity among intranet users to the fore and emphasized collaboration as one of the major benefits of an intranet (Bejune 2007; Dworak and Jeffrey 2009; Kennedy and Dysart 2007). Some libraries created their own custom systems to include Web 2.0 features in an intranet (Engard and Park 2006), while others chose off-the-shelf content management systems (Solomon 2006; Herrera 2008; Houghton-Jan and Staley 2008; Kammerer 2009). Microsoft SharePoint is one of the off-the-shelf intranet solutions and includes many out-of-the-box Web 2.0 tools. Among content management solutions used for intranets, SharePoint is the one that a plurality of organizations (48 percent) implemented to deploy Web 2.0 tools inside the firewall, according to the recent Intranet 2.0 Global Survey (Mills 2010).

Successful intranet implementation processes using SharePoint have been described before (Rao 2003; Herrera 2008; Kammerer 2009). However, there is little discussion in the library literature about the cases of unsuccessful SharePoint implementation and adoption as discussed in this article. Also, although many articles discussed the role of organizational and social factors in the context of early intranets, how such organizational and social factors influence employees' adoption of Intranet 2.0 has received little attention.

Jan Damsgaard and Rens Scheepers (1999) observed that an intranet is initially shaped by an existing organizational structure, although it can bring about organizational changes once it is institutionalized. For this reason, intranet implementers have to rely on persuasion, management support, etc. to sell the intranet to potential adopters (338). Organizational and social factors such as subsidy and mobilization from management are crucial in the early stages of intranet implementation. Similarly, the importance of user engagement in successful intranet implementation was observed in early intranets (Duckworth 2000; Hall 2001).

More recently, Zahid Hussain, Andrew Taylor, and Donal Flynn (2004) investigated a case in which organizational and social issues—senior management's skepticism about the intranet project and the low IT-literacy of workers—made the diffusion of an intranet challenging. They analyzed how an integrated set of actions was performed over a three-year period to obtain legitimation for an intranet from its stakeholders using Structuration Theory and highlighted legitimation as a significant factor in information systems failure. On the other hand, Antonella Martini, Mariano Corso, and Luisa Pellegrini (2009) focused on the governance—the organizational choices that determine the division of the responsibilities and the key criteria to be followed in the planning and management of an intranet initiative—and its crucial role in intranet implementation, adoption, and evolution. However, neither Web 2.0 tools nor Intranet 2.0 was treated as a major topic in these studies.

BACKGROUND

The FIU Medical Library is a small library with four full-time professional librarians, two full-time and three part-time paraprofessionals, and three student assistants. The library and its governing body, the FIU College of Medicine (COM), both opened in fall 2009. In fall 2008, during the college's preparation period, the COM Information Technology (IT) department purchased Microsoft Office SharePoint Server (MOSS) 2007 Enterprise Edition and installed the system on its local server. This created the bare-bones COM SharePoint intranet. After system installation, the COM IT department contacted individual college departments, such as Finance and Human Resources, and offered help in structuring and organizing each department's intranet as a sub-site of the COM SharePoint intranet. At the time, just like the college, the library was recruiting its staff and had no content for the brand-new intranet.

SharePoint 2007 is a one-package solution for an intranet that includes not only a powerful document management feature but also many different Web 2.0 tools, such as blogs, wikis, RSS, and discussion forums. Microsoft released the first version of SharePoint, named SharePoint Team Services, in 2001. This first version allowed a user to create, author, and administer team Web sites to help a team organize and advance on a project (Rao 2003, 135). Microsoft has improved SharePoint over time. The third and most recent SharePoint product on the market is SharePoint 2007, and the next version, SharePoint 2010, is currently in beta (Microsoft 2009b).

There are three different editions of SharePoint 2007 for an intranet: Windows SharePoint Services 3.0 (WSS), MOSS 2007 Standard Edition, and MOSS 2007 Enterprise Edition. WSS is included in Windows Server 2003 as a free download, while MOSS has to be purchased separately. MOSS Standard Edition includes features not available in WSS, such as portals and enterprise search (Microsoft 2009a). MOSS Enterprise Edition adds more features to MOSS Standard Edition, such as business intelligence dashboards and the business data catalog (Wallis 2007; Microsoft 2010). Organizations may implement and use SharePoint 2007's different capabilities depending on their needs.

The most commonly implemented feature of SharePoint 2007 is its group workspace for collaboration called a "team site." Team sites are included in all three editions of SharePoint 2007. Although the FIU Medical Library intranet was implemented using MOSS Enterprise Edition, it used mostly the team site feature.

THE STRUCTURE AND THE INITIAL USE OF FIU MEDICAL LIBRARY INTRANET

To create the library space in the new COM SharePoint intranet, the digital access librarian met with the system administrator of the IT department in December 2008. Since the library was not yet fully operational, there were no established staff workflows. This made structuring the library intranet challenging. In the absence of established workflows, the digital access librarian consulted with two other librarians. The head knowledge resources development librarian and the head learning and information services librarian requested five different intranet pages based upon the library's organizational structure and service areas. As a result, the FIU Medical Library intranet was created with the following seven pages: the library intranet homepage, cataloging and collections, digital access services, education, help desk, interlibrary loan, and reference. (See Figure 1 and Figure 2.)

Microsoft SharePoint 2007 allows a user to create an intranet site by quickly selecting one of the five pre-defined templates: team site, blank site, wiki site, document workspace, or blog. The library selected the team site template for its intranet. The team site template can include various functional modules—called "Web parts" in SharePoint terminology (Microsoft 2010)—and also other types of sites such as a wiki site or a blog.

FIGURE 1 FIU Medical Library intranet—home page. Printed with the permission of FIU College of Medicine.

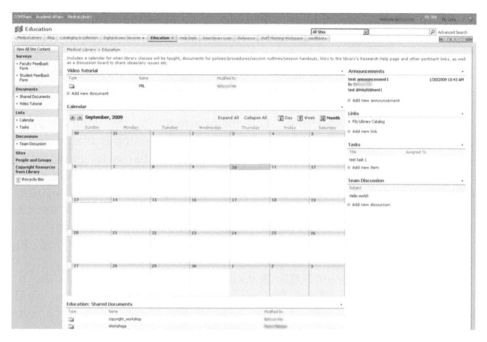

FIGURE 2 FIU Medical Library intranet—education page. Printed with the permission of FIU College of Medicine.

All library intranet pages were given the following Web parts: announcement, link, document library, and discussion forum. Some pages were also given the calendar, picture library, survey, task, and RSS viewer Web parts. All staff were given the permission setting of contributors. This enabled them to not only view but also add and update intranet content themselves.

As soon as it was structured, the intranet was used for two projects that required close collaboration and frequent communication among the four librarians: deciding on and writing all library policies for the new library and deciding on the structure, content, and design of the library's public Web site. Both projects lasted about six months, during which time the intranet was heavily used. For policy writing, a document library Web part was created in the library intranet homepage. (See Figure 3.) In this document library, named Library Policies, all policy drafts and updated versions were saved. For the library Web site project, a wiki site named *medlibbeta* was created. (See Figure 4.) Inside this wiki, multiple pages were created to hold the content of each library Web page for feedback and revision.

Although all library staff could add and modify content in the intranet, only the two librarians experienced with blogging software and wiki sites actually contributed content. The other two librarians viewed content on the intranet but provided feedback and comments via e-mail rather than posting them directly on the intranet. The communication and discussion

FIGURE 3 Document library—library policies. Printed with the permission of FIU College of Medicine.

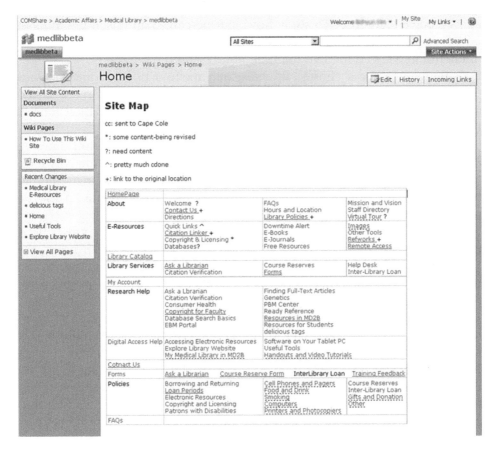

FIGURE 4 SharePoint wiki for the library Web site project—*medlibbeta*. Printed with the permission of FIU College of Medicine.

took place actively via e-mail, but the discussion forum in the intranet was left unused. Once the documents had been reviewed and revised after all librarians' feedback and comments, updated documents were uploaded to the intranet by the two experienced librarians.

Eventually, 29 files and 56 wiki pages were created and saved in the document library and the *medlibbeta* wiki site. Considering that these documents and wiki pages were for only two projects run by no more than four participants, this usage level indicates the library intranet was actively used during the library planning stage.

INTERVIEW RESULTS

Although the FIU Medical Library intranet was actively used during the initial library planning stage, its use decreased significantly after that. The staff used document libraries to store and share documents and other files. But most other Web 2.0 tools—announcements, links, tasks, and discussion forums, etc.—received little use. To study how staff perceived and used the intranet and to gather the staff's feedback on its functionality, the digital access librarian interviewed the five full-time library staff.

Interviewing was chosen as a research method because interviewees can freely elaborate on their experiences and views. Each interview lasted about an hour. The part-time staff were excluded because of their limited exposure to the library intranet.

Interview questions consisted of six different sections: previous intranet experience and training, the perception of the intranet as a productivity tool, familiarity and satisfaction with individual Web parts of the intranet, intranet use, further training needs, and other suggestions. (See Appendix A for the interview questionnaire.)

According to the interview results, only two staff members had used an intranet system at their previous workplaces. However, both noted the intranet was different from the intranets they had used in the past, which did not allow them to directly add or change content and provided no Web 2.0 tools.

Three librarians among the five full-time library staff were introduced to the bare-bones COM SharePoint intranet right after the COM IT department had set it up. No organization-wide training was offered by the IT department. The digital access librarian was not yet hired at that time, and the library intranet did not yet exist. By trial and error, the three librarians taught themselves some of the SharePoint features, such as "My Site." In contrast, two paraprofessionals were hired after the library intranet was fully structured. They were introduced to the library intranet during their orientation and received one-hour, one-on-one training from the digital access librarian about all the available features of the intranet.

Although the staff mostly used one feature of the intranet—the document library—their satisfaction with the intranet was high. The interviewees were asked to rate how satisfied they were with the intranet on a scale of 1 (least satisfied) to 10 (most satisfied). The average rating was 7.5, and two interviewees gave a 10. On the other hand, the staff regarded the intranet to be less than essential to their work. The average rating of how essential the intranet was for work was 4.6 on a scale of 1 (not at all essential) to 10 (most essential). Only one staff member gave a rating of 10.

The frequency of the staff's library intranet visits varied depending on the visit's purpose. With all purposes included, two of the five staff members visited the intranet many times a day. The other three staff visited the intranet once a day, once a week, and once a month, respectively. For the purpose of locating particular information, however, no one visited the intranet many times a day: two staff visited the intranet once a day, two once a week, and one once a month. The staff visited the intranet to add or update content even less frequently: two staff visited the intranet once a day, one once a week, and two once a month. (See Table 1.)

TABLE 1 Responses to Interview Question: How Often Do You Visit the Library Intranet?

	Frequency			
Purpose	Many times a day	Once a day	Once a week	Once a month
In general	2	1	1	1
To find information	0	2	2	1
To add or change content	0	2	1	2

The staff found the SharePoint intranet relatively easy to use, with an average rating of 3.8 on a scale from 1 (very easy) to 10 (most difficult). While two staff members rated the intranet 1 (very easy), two gave a rating of 6.

All respondents picked the document library tool as the most often used library intranet tool. It was also the only tool that all staff members had used at least once. (See Table 2.) All interviewees were familiar and satisfied with the document library tool. (See Table 3.) The second most widely used tool was the calendar. Four of five staff members had used the calendar and were familiar with it; however, the staff members were less satisfied with the calendar than the document library tool.

The staff members were much less familiar with other tools. Only one staff member had used the survey tool, and two had used the task, discussion forum, and links tools. Even those who tried these tools commented that they had used them only once either during the initial training or for testing purposes.

All interviewees ranked the document library tool, which allowed them to easily store and share files, as the best tool. As the worst feature, two staff

TABLE 2 Responses to Interview Question: Have You Used a Particular Tool in the Library Intranet?

Tool	Number of staff with the experience of using the tool	
	Never used	Used
Calendar	1	4
Document library	0	5
Announce	2	3
Survey	4	1
Task	3	2
Forum	3	2
Links	3	2

members picked the calendar tool and said it was not only cumbersome to use but also did not work well with Microsoft Outlook, the e-mail client that all staff used.

As an open-ended question, staff were also asked what communication medium they used to share information or news items with other staff. They all responded that they used e-mail because of its convenience and ease of use. No staff had used the intranet for communication purposes. As an additional communication channel, three staff members responded that they had occasionally used Microsoft Office Communicator, an instant messenger program installed on all COM staff computers.

The staff found several features of the SharePoint library intranet problematic. They pointed out the Microsoft-centric features of SharePoint 2007 as the source of the most frustrating experiences with the intranet. Some features of SharePoint do not fully work in Web browsers other than Microsoft Internet Explorer (IE). In non-IE Web browsers, the integration with Microsoft Office fails, and the WYSWYG editor in the SharePoint Web parts disappears without displaying any warning. In addition, the staff made the following comments:

TABLE 3 Responses to Interview Question: How Familiar and Satisfied Are You with Each Tool in the Library Intranet? Rate from 1 (Least Familiar/Satisfied) to 10 (Most Familiar/Satisfied)

Individual tool	Rating	
	Familiar	Satisfied
Calendar	7.8	5.2
Document library	8.8	9.2
Announce	6	6
Survey	8	9
Task	6	1
Forum	3.5	3.5
Links	8.5	7.5

- individual Web parts do not work in an intuitive way,
- the Web parts require users to perform many unnecessary clicks,
- the SharePoint document library tool does not allow simultaneous editing by multiple people,
- the calendar tool does not work well with Microsoft Outlook,
- the library intranet URL is too long to remember, and
- locating something in the library intranet is not always easy.

Three staff members showed interest in future training, and hands-on training was the preferred training method. Documentation, with many screenshots and video tutorials, was also suggested as a means of support. Two staff members indicated that they had no need for further SharePoint training. The cited reasons were the intranet being unnecessary to work and the familiarity with most of the SharePoint intranet features respectively.

All staff were satisfied with the current organization of the library intranet by tabs. However, one staff member commented that many Web parts in the library intranet homepage made the page look busy. Three staff members were using the custom Web browser toolbar (see Figure 5), which the digital

FIGURE 5 Custom toolbar for the FIU Medical Library SharePoint intranet. Printed with the permission of FIU College of Medicine.

access librarian created specifically for quick access to the different pages of the intranet, and found it useful. Two staff members were not aware of the toolbar but wanted to install it.

DISCUSSION AND ANALYSIS

Intranet as a File Repository

The interview results raised more questions than answers. The satisfaction rating was high, yet the staff had not used most of the tools in the library intranet and regarded it as non-essential to their work and communication. According to the interview results, the staff also found the intranet relatively easy to use. So, questions remain: with what aspect of the intranet were staff satisfied? Why do staff not use more tools on the intranet?

The document library feature of the intranet may explain these seemingly contradictory responses. The staff needed a file repository that would allow them to share and store files. The document library tool met this need. It also enabled the staff to control access to files with sophisticated permission settings, so that individual documents or folders can be shared with people outside the library. This is why the staff were quite satisfied with the intranet. Since one intranet tool satisfactorily met the staff members' most prominent need, the overall satisfaction with the intranet itself was high.

During the interviews, library staff also preferred the intranet and its document library tool over the library's shared network drives because it was easier to access files on the intranet than those on the network drives from home. However, they regarded the intranet as non-essential to work because the document library tool had an alternative (i.e., shared network drives). This shows the staff almost equated the intranet with one tool they used and were satisfied with.

Web 2.0 Tools for Internal Communication

While the document library tool works as a file repository, the underused Web 2.0 tools in the library intranet were meant to facilitate internal communication. The announcement tool obviates the need to e-mail the entire staff to announce library-related news. The discussion forum tool allows the staff to have a discussion in one place and to archive the posts for later reference. The task tool is useful for the staff on the same project to update one another about the progress of their assigned tasks. Using the link tool, the staff can share links to interesting Web content without sending e-mails to the entire staff.

The staff, however, continued to use e-mail for all communication needs. E-mail was already established as a legitimate and acceptable communication channel at the library, and staff were familiar and comfortable with it. Also, there was no mandate or encouragement from management to use the intranet tools. Staff were given no compelling reason to invest their time and efforts in learning how to use unfamiliar new tools. The new tools' availability and ease of use did little to motivate the staff. The opportunity to improve internal communication using the intranet was missed because the need for more efficient internal communication was not clearly presented to and perceived by the library as a whole.

Staff Expectations

The interview results also showed that staff expectations for the intranet's potential abilities were very high. The staff did not find the tools provided in the intranet difficult to use. Rather, they were keen to comment on those tools' limitations.

As previously mentioned, staff were disappointed by SharePoint's lack of support for non-IE Web browsers, its awkward interface for the Web parts, its failure to work seamlessly with Microsoft Outlook Calendar, its long URLs for SharePoint pages, and the difficulty of locating information in it. In addition, since the intranet was built with a template and looked almost like a public Web site, some staff were disappointed by the fact that the intranet was not as visually attractive as public Web sites. It is possible to create a custom style for a team site in SharePoint 2007, but it requires additional programming. A custom style for departmental sub-sites in the COM intranet was not a high priority task for the COM IT department, because those intranet sites were viewed and used internally and not by the public.

The staff also wanted the intranet to provide features that were equal to those found in comparable tools freely available on the Web. For example, they compared the document library tool with a similar free service, Google Docs, and asked why SharePoint, a purchased solution, lacked the feature that Google Docs offers, i.e., simultaneous document editing. As intranet users become more familiar and comfortable with various tools freely available on the Web and as intranets incorporate similar tools, they are likely to expect their intranets to provide the same level of user experience that they get from the Internet. It is possible for the future versions of SharePoint to include simultaneous editing of the document library and also to resolve the other issues mentioned in this section. However, the problems that staff observed with SharePoint will remain as long as the intranet is based upon SharePoint 2007.

Barriers to Intranet Adoption

The implementation of the FIU Medical Library intranet was successful only in the respect that it addressed the staff's need for file sharing and storing.

The intranet failed to be used in other areas, such as internal communication and collaboration. Most of the Web 2.0 tools that were meant to improve efficiency in these areas failed to attract much attention from the staff and received little use.

It is clear from the interview results that technological barriers were not what hindered the staff's adoption of these Web 2.0 tools. Rather, the major barrier to the intranet adoption was the lack of organizational effort and encouragement. Martini et al. (2009) pointed out that there was a tendency for management to manage an intranet implementation project from a purely technical perspective without systematically facing its organizational and change management aspects, and that this often led to the inertia of an intranet after implementation. This was the case with the FIU COM intranet and its sub-site, the FIU Medical Library intranet.

The FIU COM intranet was regarded as a project of the COM IT department, and as such, it was introduced as an optional technology. There was no strategic planning for either the FIU COM intranet or FIU Medical Library intranet. Staff training for the new SharePoint system had been minimal, until the digital access librarian learned various functionalities of SharePoint at a one-on-one meeting with the COM IT department's system administrator. After creating the library intranet with the help of the COM IT department, the digital access librarian saw a need for SharePoint training and provided training for the staff. However, there was no official mandate or encouragement from the management to learn how to use the FIU COM intranet or the library intranet.

The approach taken to the implementation of the FIU COM intranet and Medical Library intranet stands in sharp contrast with the SharePoint intranet implementation cases at the University of Mississippi (UM) Libraries and at the Community Medical Center Library described by Kevin Herrera (2008) and Judith J. Kammerer (2009), respectively. The SharePoint intranet of the UM Libraries was introduced through a form of strategic planning (Herrera 2008). Although the intranet project at the UM Libraries was led by the IT department, just as it was at the FIU COM, there were conversations between the IT department manager and the other department managers about which potential features of the intranet were likely to be widely used. Although these conversations were informal, they generated interest about the new intranet system among the department managers who were major stakeholders of the new intranet project. The UM Libraries' intranet was also deployed through multiple stages of training. Training sessions provided opportunities for library employees to become familiar with the new system. While the departmental training sessions throughout the UM Libraries were underway, the IT department responded to requests for separate training sessions that focused on particular SharePoint tools in which the staff were interested. The UM Libraries' intranet succeeded in obtaining a critical mass of users and content in a short time by first engaging department managers with the features of the new intranet system and their potential uses and then by providing more training for the libraries' staff about the intranet. As a result, the intranet met existing and clearly perceived needs.

Kammerer (2009) described a SharePoint intranet implementation case very similar to that of the FIU Medical Library. As in the FIU Medical Library intranet, the Community Medical Center Library's intranet was created as a sub-site of a larger organizational intranet, and the library relied on the Medical Center IT department for its intranet implementation. Unlike the FIU Medical Library, however, the Community Medical Center Library benefited from the strategic planning by the center's IT department. This strategic planning resulted in the creation of an "education content" team supported by the nursing CEO. The education content team consisted of key personnel who represented various hospital areas including the library, which delivered medical information to physicians, nurses, and other professional staff. In other words, the Community Medical Center took the collaborative approach of linking multiple departments to the task of organizing online educational content and services and of migrating them to the new intranet system. The library participated in this process, forming partnerships with other departments and individuals that performed educational services similar to those of the library.

On the other hand, the FIU Medical Library staff were allowed to adopt or not adopt the library intranet based upon their personal preferences and choices because of the lack of organizational efforts to promote and encourage the staff's use of the new system. This made it difficult for the FIU Medical Library intranet to obtain a critical mass of users and content, which is one of the crucial stages in the evolution of an intranet (Damsgaard and Scheepers 2000). The low use of the library intranet resulted in little useful information in it; the little information in the intranet again discouraged employees from taking time to participate in and contribute more useful information to the intranet. Even though a few staff members had been initially enthusiastic about the library intranet, without proper organizational encouragement and other staff members joining the intranet, they became less active. Consequently, the intranet became stagnant.

It should also be noted that, in the case of the FIU Medical Library, there had been neither a previous intranet nor any content to be migrated from the old intranet to the new one as the library was brand new. The lack of pre-existing useful content for the library intranet is likely to have slowed the staff's adoption, because creating new content requires more time and effort than simply migrating or updating existing content.

The case of the FIU Medical Library intranet highlights common challenges in intranet implementation at small libraries. Often, small libraries do not have a dedicated IT department and lack sufficient resources and funding to design and implement their own intranets. A small library's intranet is likely to be a sub-site of a larger intranet that belongs to the library's governing body. If the top management of an organization views an intranet project as a purely technological one, it is likely that the intranet will be implemented without much strategic planning or organization-wide efforts to promote and mandate its use. In such a case, it is particularly difficult for an individual department, such as a library, to persuade their staff to adopt the new intranet system. In the absence of organization-wide activities to establish an intranet as a common platform for communication and collaboration, it is difficult to motivate employees with a compelling reason to learn and use new and unfamiliar tools.

CONCLUSION

For staff, an intranet is another new technology to learn. In order for an intranet to be successfully adopted, the tools it provides should be easy to use and must meet existing needs better than old and familiar tools do, thereby effectively streamlining daily workflows and improving collaboration. The needs an intranet can meet may well be latent, and both management and employees may not even realize that such needs exist. In such a case, making latent needs explicit to both management and staff must precede an actual intranet implementation process. Intranets can also meet additional needs that may arise in the future. Also, the needs may not justify the adoption of new and unfamiliar technology unless the majority of the staff adopt and consistently use the new technology. Even when the intranet is easy to use and its tools can better serve existing needs, the staff may still be reluctant to change. Therefore, strong incentives are necessary to motivate employees to adopt new tools until a critical mass of users and content is obtained.

Organizational and social factors are important in intranet implementation because these incentives are often provided in the form of organization-wide strategic planning, training, and promotion. Employees are also more likely to adopt an intranet if its use is officially encouraged and sometimes mandated by management, as a mandate provides employees with a compelling reason to adopt the intranet (Guenther 2006; Fichter 2006).

Both early intranets and Intranet 2.0 share the goal of improving organizational performance and efficiency by facilitating internal communication, knowledge and information sharing, and collaboration. But Intranet 2.0 aims at engaging users with Web 2.0 tools that enable employees to freely interact with one another and to contribute content to an intranet rather than centrally aggregating and disseminating information.

It is important to note that Web 2.0 tools are social in nature. For this reason, their value lies entirely in the employee's actual use of those tools. Web 2.0 tools can strengthen existing social relationships among employees and consequently facilitate and improve their communication, information and knowledge sharing, and collaboration at an organization level. However,

Web 2.0 tools themselves neither create nor foster social relationships, nor can they thrive in an environment where the interaction among users and their active participation are neither promoted nor encouraged.

The case of the FIU Medical Library's SharePoint intranet shows that the availability of Web 2.0 tools and their ease of use are not sufficient to motivate staff to adopt Intranet 2.0. With many off-the-shelf intranet solutions like SharePoint, setting up an Intranet 2.0 system becomes a relatively easy technological task. However, the availability of Web 2.0 tools in an intranet itself does not make the most crucial part of intranet implementation—persuading and motivating employees to adopt and use the intranet—any easier. The successful implementation of Intranet 2.0 requires the same level of thorough planning and organizational efforts to make intranets before Web 2.0 succeed. Intranet 2.0 also faces the new challenge of satisfying users' high expectations that often result from their everyday experience with free Web 2.0 tools on the Web.

REFERENCES

Bejune, Matthew M. 2007. Wikis in libraries. *Information Technology and Libraries* 26(3): 26–38.

Damsgaard, Jan, and Rens Scheepers. 1999. Power, influence and intranet implementation. A safari of South African organizations. *Information Technology and People* 12(4): 333–358.

———. 2000. Managing the crises in intranet implementation: A stage model. *Information Systems Journal* 10(2): 131–149.

Duckworth, Dot. 2000. What "sells" an intranet? *VINE: The Journal of Information and Knowledge Management Systems* 30(2): 33–37.

Dworak, Ellen, and Keven Jeffrey. 2009. Wiki to the rescue: Creating a more dynamic intranet. *Library Hi Tech* 27(3): 403–410.

Engard, Nicole C., and RayAna M. Park. 2006. Intranet 2.0: Fostering collaboration. *Online* 30(3): 16–23.

Fichter, Darlene. 2006. Making your intranet live up to its potential. *Online* 30(1): 51–53.

Guenther, Kim. 2006. Moving your intranet to the next level. *Online* 30(6): 55–57.

Hall, Hazel. 2001. Input-friendliness: Motivating knowledge sharing across intranets. *Journal of Information Science* 27(3): 139–146.

Herrera, Kevin. 2008. From static files to collaborative workspace with SharePoint. *Library Hi Tech* 26(1): 80–94.

Houghton-Jan, Sarah, and Shannon Staley. 2008. SharePoint for libraries: Streaming your intranet management. http://librarianinblack.net/librarianinblack/2008/10/internet-librarian-2008-sharepoint-for-libraries-streamlining-your-intranet-management.html (accessed March 9, 2010).

Hussain, Zahid, Andrew Taylor, and Donal Flynn. 2004. A case study of the process of achieving legitimation in information systems development. *Journal of Information Science* 30(5): 408–417.

Kammerer, Judith J. 2009. Migrating a hospital library Web site to SharePoint and expanding its usefulness. *Journal of Hospital Librarianship* 9(4): 408–418.

Kennedy, Mary Lee, and Jane Dysart, eds. 2007. *Intranets for info pros*. Medford, NJ: Information Today.

Martini, Antonella, Mariano Corso, and Luisa Pellegrini. 2009. An empirical roadmap for intranet evolution. *International Journal of Information Management* 29(4): 295–308.

McAfee, Andrew. 2006. Enterprise 2.0, version 2.0. http://andrewmcafee.org/2006/05/enterprise_20_version_20/ (accessed March 9, 2010).

Merono-Cerdan, Angel L., Pedro Soto-Acosta, and Carolina Lopez-Nicolas. 2008. Analyzing collaborative technologies' effect on performance through intranet use orientations. *Journal of Enterprise Information Management* 21(1): 39–51.

Microsoft. 2009a. What is SharePoint? http://sharepoint.microsoft.com/product/details/Pages/default.aspx (accessed March 9, 2010).

———. 2009b. SharePoint editions overview. http://sharepoint.microsoft.com/product/editions/Pages/default.aspx (accessed March 9, 2010).

———. 2010. Which SharePoint technology is right for you? http://office.microsoft.com/en-us/sharepointtechnology/fx101758691033.aspx (accessed March 9, 2010).

Mills, Julian. 2010. Intranet 2.0 becomes mainstream. http://www.prescientdigital.com/articles/intranet-articles/intranet-2-0-becomes-mainstream (accessed March 9, 2010).

Oberhelman, David D. 2007. Coming to terms with Web 2.0. *Reference Reviews* 21(7): 5–6.

O'Reilly, Tim. 2005. What Is Web 2.0? http://www.oreillynet.com/pub/a/oreilly/tim/news/2005/09/30/what-is-web-20.html (accessed March 9, 2010).

Rao, Abhijit. 2003. Using Microsoft SharePoint Team Services for library committee management. *Information Technology and Libraries* 22(3): 133–137.

Solomon, Marc. 2006. Easy wins and hard lessons on intranets from a SharePoint deployment. *Searcher* 14(10): 18–25.

Wallis, Chris. 2007. What's the point? Next-generation legal information systems and Microsoft Sharepoint: Contender or pretender? *Legal Information Management* 7(4): 268–271.

APPENDIX A

INTERVIEW QUESTIONNAIRE

Each rating question was given a rating scale of 1 (least) to 10 (most).

Previous experience with an intranet and training:

- Initially, how were you introduced to the library SharePoint intranet when you started work?
- What kind of experience did you have with an intranet system previously?

- What kind of training was provided for using SharePoint?
- What did you think about SP initially?

The library intranet as a productivity tool:

- How satisfied are you overall with the library intranet as a workplace productivity tool?
- How difficult would it be to do your work if you cannot use the library intranet?
- In your opinion, what is the most useful feature of the library intranet?
- In your opinion, what is the least useful feature of the library intranet?
- Based upon the initial expectation you had about the library intranet, how satisfied are you with the intranet?

Individual tools in the library intranet:

• How familiar are you with the Calendar Tool?	• How satisfied are you with the Calendar Tool?
• How familiar are you with the Document Library Tool?	• How satisfied are you with the Document Library Tool?
• How familiar are you with the Announcement Tool?	• How satisfied are you with the Announcement Tool?
• How familiar are you with the Survey Tool?	• How satisfied are you with the Survey Tool?
• How familiar are you with the Tasks Tool?	• How satisfied are you with the Tasks Tool?
• How familiar are you with the Discussion Forum Tool?	• How satisfied are you with the Discussion Forum Tool?
• How familiar are you with the Links Tool?	• How satisfied are you with the Links Tool?

Which tool do you use most often in the SP intranet?

- How intuitive is the way each tool works to you? Rate from 1 (least intuitive) to 10 (most intuitive).
- Are there any other tools that you would like? If so, please describe.

Use of the library intranet:

- How often do you check the library intranet? For example, many times a day, once a day, a couple of times a week, once a week, once a month or less.
- How often do you go to the library intranet to find information? For example, many times a day, once a day, a couple of times a week, once a week, once a month or less.
- How often do you go to the library intranet to contribute or make changes? For example, many times a day, once a day, a couple of times a week, once a week, once a month or less.

- How easy or difficult do you find to use the library intranet overall?
- When you have something to share with other library staff, what communication medium do you use? For example, e-mail alone, e-mail and the library intranet, the library intranet alone, MS Office Communicator, other. What are the reasons for using that communication medium?
- What do you think makes the library staff use a communication medium other than the intranet?
- What would make you and other staff use the intranet for collaboration more?

Training needs:

- If you have received any training about the library intranet, how satisfied were you with the training?
- Do you have any suggestions that you think may improve the training?
- Do you think you would benefit from more training on how to use the library intranet?
- If so, what kind of format would you like the training to be? For example, hands-on training, online slides, or video tutorial.
- Any other suggestions on training?

Intranet structure and suggestions:

- Did you find all library intranet pages created for your service area satisfactory?
- How would you improve the way the current library intranet is organized?
- Are there any features you would like to see in the intranet? If so, please describe.
- Did you have any particularly frustrating experience with the SP intranet? If so, please describe.

An Unexpected Ally: Using Microsoft's SharePoint to Create a Departmental Intranet

DAVID DAHL

Albert S. Cook Library, Towson University, Towson, Maryland, USA

In September 2008, the Albert S. Cook Library at Towson University implemented an intranet to support the various functions of the library's Reference Department. This intranet is called the RefPortal. After exploring open source options and other Web 2.0 tools, the department (under the guidance of the library technology coordinator) chose Microsoft Windows SharePoint Services 3.0, a proprietary product, as their intranet platform. Various components of SharePoint fulfill the Reference Department's needs, which include recording reference transactions, publishing policies and procedures, and sharing pertinent information at the reference desk. Several lessons and best practices have emerged since the department's initial SharePoint implementation. A survey of reference staff indicates satisfaction with the RefPortal, but more training is needed for the portal to be used to its maximum potential. Staff use of the portal has served as an example for other departments in the library and for the university. In the future, the Reference Department plans to explore unused SharePoint components to solve additional departmental needs and to continually assess and maintain the existing implementation.

THE NEED FOR A DEPARTMENTAL INTRANET

The Albert S. Cook Library at Towson University in the northern Baltimore suburb of Towson, MD, serves a student population of more than 21,000. The library supports the research needs of the university's students, faculty, and staff and provides basic library services for the Towson community. Along with traditional library services, Cook Library also houses other university services, such as academic tutoring, technology services, and copy-and-print services. The library is supported by a staff of 53 employees and more than 60 part-time student workers. The Reference Department consists of fourteen full-time reference librarians, one full-time library associate, one contractual evening reference librarian, and one residency librarian, who rotates between several departments throughout his/her two-year residency. At Towson, librarians serve on university and library committees, teach information literacy sessions, and perform various other functions that require their time in buildings around campus.

Reference shifts are scheduled on a weekly basis, so desk hours vary from week to week. While the library associate spends an average of four hours per weekday at the reference desk, and the evening reference librarian covers most weekday evening shifts, the rotating of reference shifts among librarians can lead to disconnects in communication from one shift to the next. It is entirely possible for two librarians to go several weeks without physically seeing each other. This working environment for the Reference Department staff makes it imperative to establish good lines of communication and collaboration in order to work effectively and efficiently as a department. A method was needed to facilitate the dissemination of information relevant to librarians' shifts on the reference desk, to store and retrieve policies and procedures, and to collaborate asynchronously on documents.

Before the implementation of the RefPortal, most communication and collaboration needs were addressed through several independent tools. E-mail was most often used to communicate important announcements and facilitate departmental discussions, a shared network drive was used to store documents, and a binder containing policies and procedures was kept at the reference desk. Additionally, the number and type of reference transactions per day were kept in paper format and later transcribed into Excel for the library's annual report. These tools caused information overload, irretrievable files and multiple versions of documents, outdated policies and procedural information, and inefficient use of resources to convert data into an electronic format. The various locations of and methods for retrieving information did not effectively meet the Reference Department's needs. The department needed a centralized location—resembling an intranet—that would provide access to all departmental communication and information.

CHOOSING A PLATFORM

Several options were available for creating or selecting a tool that would serve as the departmental intranet, each requiring varying amounts of time, money, and skills to implement. The platform needed to support the basic functions of an intranet, providing "efficient communication" and a location for "archiving important information" (Benzing 1998, 54). Additionally, it needed to closely match the workflows of the department and the specific functions that had been completed with disparate tools.

Many organizations have taken advantage of Web 2.0 technologies and principles to create more effective intranets. These tools support the "social nature of work" (Holtz 2008, 16). Libraries have generally been early adopters of Web 2.0 for both external and internal purposes. Matthew Bejune (2007) found that 31.4 percent of 33 identified wikis were used for library staff collaboration. San Diego State University Library moved their intranet to a wiki, which increased staff's "ability to update content" (Dworak and Jeffery 2009, 409). The collaborative nature of wikis makes them suitable as tools for creating and maintaining procedural and training documentation (Welsh 2007).

Blogs have been identified as useful Web 2.0 tools for supporting internal communication. Alison McIntyre and Janette Nicolle (2008) found that "internal blogs have the potential to develop a stronger sense of community" (686). While both wiki and blogging software would be relatively simple to implement, it was not believed that either fully offered the desired functionality for the department's intranet. However, a wiki was identified as a potential solution to replace the policies and procedures binder, and a tool resembling the functionality of a blog could be used to post announcements. The need for something more than what any one Web 2.0 tool could provide left the library with three main options: a custom-built intranet, an open-source solution that would support all required functions, or a proprietary intranet product.

Building an intranet in-house could have potentially produced a solution that would most closely match the department's needs and workflows, since the application could be written to match these requirements. Nicole C. Engard and RayAna Park (2006) discussed Jenkins Law Library's implementation of a homegrown intranet using PHP and MySQL. Similar to the needs of Jenkins Law Library, Cook Library's Reference Department wanted "more than just a wiki" (18). However, the time, server space, and programming needed to create and host a homegrown intranet did not fit the department's timeline and available resources.

Open source solutions that could fulfill the functions of an intranet were also evaluated. While Engard and Park's (2006) implementation of a homegrown intranet indicates that some libraries are creating these types of solutions, publishing these solutions as open source software for others to use does not appear to be common. During the evaluation period, no library intranet solutions were available at SourceForge.net (http://sourceforge.net), one of the largest Web sites for posting open source software.

Since existing open source library intranet solutions were not available, the department explored the use of a content management system (CMS) as a potential open source solution for creating a portal. Several libraries, including Darien Public Library (Darien, CT), have recently begun using open source CMSs such as Drupal (http://drupal.org) as a platform to manage Web content (Sheehan 2009). While most discussions of CMS implementations focus on their use for managing a library's external site, the same type of system has potential as an intranet platform as well. A CMS can be secured, requiring individual logins and assigned permissions; it allows any user (with permissions) to add, delete, or update content; and most CMSs include common Web 2.0 tools.

As a proponent of open source software, the author and other evaluators of the department's intranet solution strongly considered an open source CMS. The openness of a CMS like Drupal would allow the department to customize the portal's design and integrate customized, locally built modules into the CMS platform. However, two reasons led to the department choosing a different option for an intranet. First, most of the well-supported open-source CMSs are built on a Linux platform using PHP, but the library runs Windows Server 2003 on an IIS server. While it is possible to run a PHP-built CMS on an IIS server, it usually requires several workarounds and more maintenance. Second, an open source CMS is typically designed with enough flexibility to support a wide variety of uses. While this is generally one of the benefits of a CMS, the flexibility would also require that the department spend more time planning and designing the intranet. Ultimately, a solution like SharePoint, which would function as an intranet "out of the box," fit the department's needs more closely.

Using proprietary software was, admittedly, the least desired option by those library staff evaluating available options. The term "proprietary" often connotes expensive, inflexible software that cannot be customized to a particular user's or institution's needs, whereas "open source" is often defined as being useable "by anyone free of license fees, with access to the source code via the Internet, and [containing] the ability to share additions/modifications with others" (van Rooij 2007, 439). Initially, it did not seem possible for an out-of-the-box proprietary solution to match the department's intranet needs and meet the desire for an inexpensive solution. However, after investigating several potential answers, Microsoft's Windows SharePoint Services (WSS) 3.0 (http://office.microsoft.com/en-us/sharepointtechnology) emerged as the best solution. In contrast to the common perception of proprietary software, WSS 3.0 is a free component of Windows Server 2003 or 2008. Additionally, the university was beginning to explore SharePoint, allowing the Reference Department to take advantage of the university's implementation and avoid the need to set up and host SharePoint on its own server. In addition to WSS, the university also purchased Microsoft Office SharePoint Server (MOSS) 2007, which extends the functionality of WSS. Towson University also has a site license for Microsoft Office 2007, including SharePoint Designer, and uses SQL Server 2005 as a back-end database for their SharePoint

TABLE 1 Components of a SharePoint Solution

Software	Functions	Cost and requirement
Windows Sharepoint Services (WSS) 3.0	Collaboration, content management, RSS, wikis, blogs, master pages, calendars, surveys, mobile views	Required Free
Microsoft Office SharePoint Server 2007 (MOSS 2007)	Search, page layouts, LDAP, SSO, slide libraries, repository, social networking	Optional $$$
Microsoft Office (2007)	Use Office applications from within SharePoint	Required $$$
SQL Server 2005	Back-end database	Required $$$
Microsoft SharePoint Designer 2007	Create Web parts, master pages, CSS, customize sites	Optional $$$

implementation. Table 1 lists the various required and optional components needed to run a SharePoint solution. While the library's Reference Department takes advantage of some of the extended functionality in MOSS 2007, the SharePoint solution and features described in this article consist of WSS 3.0, Microsoft Office 2007, and SQL Server 2005.

The SharePoint line of portal solutions was first released in 2001 under the name SharePoint Portal Server 2001. Since then, SharePoint products have been increasingly embraced by the corporate world, culminating in the release of WSS 3.0 and MOSS 2007 in 2007 (Michel 2008). Despite its popularity in the corporate world, documentation of its use in libraries has been minimal. University of Mississippi Libraries successfully implemented SharePoint in 2007, noting its usefulness right "out-of-the-box" (Herrera 2008, 82). SharePoint is a popular corporate solution because it offers a lot of features, though using just those features that address specific needs is recommended at the start (Gruman 2008). Web 2.0 tools, such as blogs and wikis, are available, as are more standard organizational tools like document sharing, search utilities, and issue tracking.

SharePoint fulfilled all the requirements for the department's intranet and also offered additional benefits that other solutions could not. Because it is a Microsoft product, SharePoint integrates well with Active Directory, allowing reference staff to use their university accounts with SharePoint. Intranet security and permissions could easily be established by the intranet's administrators. SharePoint also offered document management, collaboration, and searching—features the other solutions did not have. This document management system includes fluid integration with the Microsoft Office suite of applications. While open source office applications are becoming more prevalent, Towson University students, faculty, and staff are still heavy users of Microsoft Office applications. The university's implementation of SharePoint, the ability to set up SharePoint quickly and easily, and the ability to meet the Reference Department's needs with one tool made SharePoint a clear choice for the department's intranet. The intranet launched in September 2008 under the name RefPortal.

IMPLEMENTING SHAREPOINT

Once SharePoint is installed, new sites are simple to create and are limited only by the amount of server storage space available. Several templates are provided to facilitate the creation of new sites by automatically adding certain SharePoint components to the new site. A blank template is available as well. After the site is created, SharePoint components (see Figure 1) can be added, deleted, or edited. Basic SharePoint components can be renamed and customized to display particular information for various instances of the component. Once a component is added to a site, that instance of the component becomes what Microsoft calls a "Web part." Web parts are reusable pieces of content. Once added to a SharePoint site, a Web part can be used in various locations. The customization of SharePoint components and the use of Web parts to create reusable content make SharePoint a highly customizable intranet platform.

Because SharePoint was a new, highly customizable tool for the department (including those charged with the RefPortal's development), the implementation process began with the use of a beta site. This site was set up during the platform selection process, but since then, it has provided a safe place for testing and developing the design and functionality of the RefPortal without interfering with the use of the actual RefPortal. The department's beta site was set up using a "Team Site" template, which automatically included SharePoint's shared documents, announcements, links, and calendar components. A site can be further customized by selecting from various color schemes (i.e., themes) and adding a logo to the site. Though the Reference Department has not done so, SharePoint Designer can be used to customize a site beyond the options available within the SharePoint interface. Because creating new SharePoint sites is a simple process, adding a

Libraries	Communications	Tracking
Document Library	Announcements	Links
Form Library	Contacts	Calendar
Wiki Page Library	Discussion Board	Tasks
Picture Library		Project Tasks
Data Connection Library		Issue Tracking
Translation Management Library		Survey
Slide Library		

FIGURE 1 SharePoint components.

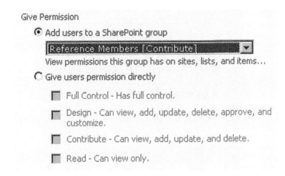

Give Permission

⊙ Add users to a SharePoint group

Reference Members [Contribute]

View permissions this group has on sites, lists, and items...

○ Give users permission directly

☐ Full Control - Has full control.

☐ Design - Can view, add, update, delete, approve, and customize.

☐ Contribute - Can view, add, update, and delete.

☐ Read - Can view only.

FIGURE 2 Assigning user groups and permissions in SharePoint.

development site for testing unused components and exploring other customizable aspects of SharePoint is highly recommended.

SharePoint allows permission levels for individuals or groups. Permissions can be set to "full control," "design," "contribute," or "read" (listed in descending order of access privileges). To best manage permissions, the department decided to set permissions for groups, allowing the site administrator to add or remove individuals from the group rather than assigning unique permissions for each individual within the department. The corresponding group names for the department include "reference owners," "reference designers," "reference members," and "reference visitors" (see Figure 2). All Reference Department staff are considered reference members, giving them the ability to access and contribute to all areas of the RefPortal. Reference visitors are other library staff who may need to view materials within the RefPortal but do not contribute or edit those materials. Two library staff—the library technology coordinator and an emerging technologies librarian—are reference owners and designers in order to perform general maintenance, add/remove features and functions, and improve the layout and organization of the SharePoint RefPortal.

The organization of the RefPortal was initially determined by the two reference owners. Navigation within the RefPortal was assigned to SharePoint's "Quick Launch" menu, a side navigation menu that provides access to all areas of the portal. SharePoint offers tabbed navigation as well, supporting global navigation. Initially, this was left unused as it was predicted that the intranet would expand to other library departments, requiring an overarching global navigation. The Quick Launch navigation is organized into categories, including resources, news, and discussions (see Figure 3). These are organized so the portal's most frequently used sections are located at the top of the list.

The RefPortal's homepage was designed to support the four main functions of the intranet, which are recording reference transaction statistics, posting announcements, storing and retrieving procedures and policies, and

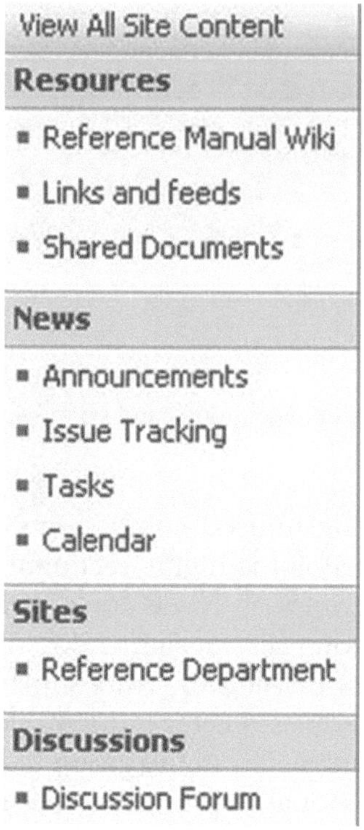

FIGURE 3 SharePoint's QuickLaunch navigation.

reporting computing and printing issues (see Figure 4). While some of these functions have their own section within the portal, the RefPortal takes advantage of SharePoint's Web parts to create an aggregate homepage that displays information for each of the portal's four main functions. Therefore, the newest changes to the Reference Manual, the latest announcements, and current issues can all be viewed from the homepage of the portal, and more information can be accessed via hyperlinks.

Recording Reference Transactions

While reference transactions could be tracked using built-in SharePoint components, the department was already in the process of developing an in-house solution for recording reference transactions (StatsTracker). As mentioned above, integration of transaction tracking was a key factor in choosing an intranet platform. Two possibilities existed for integration of the Stats-Tracker with SharePoint. The first option was to transform the Web-based StatsTracker into a customized SharePoint Web part, and the second option was to use SharePoint's Site Aggregator Web part to embed the StatsTracker. The second option proved to be far simpler. The Site Aggregator Web part allows any Web site to be embedded within SharePoint. Since the StatsTracker

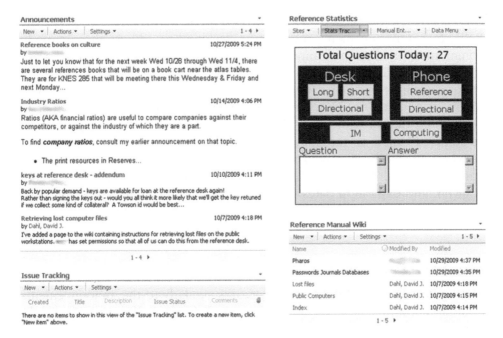

FIGURE 4 The RefPortal homepage.

was already a Web-based tool, the only needed changes were design changes to make it fit within the RefPortal homepage layout. To create a custom Web part would have required significantly more time and programming.

The Reference Manual Wiki

Converting the department's Reference Manual binder into electronic format had been discussed before SharePoint was chosen as an intranet platform. The wiki feature within SharePoint allows any member of the Reference Department to add or update content related to policies and procedures. An index and table of contents were established to facilitate browsing of the wiki. The manual can also be searched using SharePoint's integrated search engine. New wiki pages and updates to existing pages are displayed on the RefPortal's homepage, notifying members of the Reference Department when content is added or changed. Using a wiki for the Reference Manual also allows various entries to be hyperlinked to each other and provides links to external pages. Any user with reference member permissions can add, edit, or delete information in the wiki.

Posting Announcements

One of the common problems for any reference desk is communication between desk shifts. Information presented during one individual's reference shift might not be passed on to the next person working the desk. The RefPortal's announcements section was designed to address these gaps in communication. Common announcements might alert other reference desk staff of a rogue library assignment (the dreaded scavenger hunt), information about a campus event that numerous people have asked about, or a new report of potential interest. Announcements are a standard component in SharePoint, but as with other SharePoint components, the display can be customized based on the administrator's preferences. The five most recent announcements are displayed on the RefPortal homepage with a link to more announcements. The name of the individual who wrote the announcement is given, and expiration dates can be set so that timely announcements are automatically removed when the expiration date is passed.

Reporting Computing and Printing Issues

The RefPortal's Issue Tracker system works similarly to the announcements section. Its purpose is to communicate computing, printing, and other technology problems to other members of the Reference Department. E-mail alerts are also sent to those individuals responsible for the maintenance of library technology. Status updates and comments can be left as issues are resolved. Like the announcements section, the five most recent issues are displayed on the library's homepage. Additionally, a filter is used to hide technology issues that have been resolved. Issues can also be linked to previous issues, creating a knowledge base for troubleshooting computing issues.

ASSESSMENT, BEST PRACTICES, AND LESSONS LEARNED

Implementation of the RefPortal has been largely successful, as the Reference Department has readily adopted the portal. Several variables increased this early acceptance of the RefPortal as a departmental intranet. The main factor was the integration of the department's StatsTracker into SharePoint. Keeping track of reference transactions at the desk is a required activity. Since every reference member works multiple shifts at the desk each week, all staff are guaranteed to login to the RefPortal on a regular basis. This was important for encouraging use during the early stages of adoption. As staff used the StatsTracker, they gradually became familiar with other features of the portal. Displaying new content from the Reference Manual, new announcements, and computing issues on the homepage increases the portal's success as a means of communication and knowledge sharing. Any functions that are necessary for job performance will guarantee increased use of the intranet if they are strategically embedded within it.

Because it is necessary for reference staff to use the RefPortal during their reference shifts, a shortcut was created from the reference desk's computers. The shortcut made the process of getting into the RefPortal quick and easy. This shortcut offered one other significant advantage. As discovered by University of Mississippi Libraries' implementation of SharePoint, "There are some cases where functionality is impaired" by the "Microsoft-centric nature" of SharePoint (Herrera 2008, 93). This is most noticeable when using Share-Point in browsers other than Internet Explorer (IE). Tasks like document sharing and wiki editing do not work as intended outside of IE. To alleviate this issue, the shortcut to the RefPortal opens in IE by default. Several individuals have requested this shortcut for their personal workstations as well in order to avoid the difficulties that accompany using SharePoint in a browser like Firefox.

Before making the portal publicly available, several sections were pre-populated to serve as examples of the appropriate types and organization of content for each portal area. The department's library associate was largely responsible for converting existing content from the Reference Manual binder to the SharePoint wiki. The wiki's index and table of contents were established, as were guidelines and suggestions for contributing to the wiki. This was important to maintain consistency in the wiki. While wikis benefit greatly from the wisdom of the crowd, it is also possible to lose control of the wiki's organization, decreasing its effectiveness. The guidelines suggest styling options, issues to consider when naming a wiki page, providing navigation back to the index and table of contents, and considerations for the future of the wiki.

Collecting Data

A survey (see Appendix A) was conducted in January 2009 to discover department members' comfort level and satisfaction with the RefPortal. Share-Point offers a built-in survey component for creating customized surveys. The survey was built using a combination of question types, including checkboxes, Likert scales for rating aspects of the portal, and text boxes for additional comments. SharePoint automatically aggregates the survey results and facilitates the exporting of results into Microsoft Excel.

Of the thirteen Reference Department staff eligible to take the survey in January, ten participated (77 percent). The results (available from the author) indicated most individuals (at least 50 percent) were using the four main components of the RefPortal (StatsTracker, Announcements, Reference Manual, and Issue Tracker) on at least a weekly basis. The StatsTracker and Reference Manual were seen as the most important components of the RefPortal. Seventy percent of users reported feeling comfortable using the RefPortal, but half felt they had not received adequate training. The results and additional comments indicate most department staff feel the RefPortal has potential and is an important tool for the department's work.

Learning from Mistakes

The survey results indicate that more training was necessary for Reference Department staff to be empowered to fulfill the potential of the RefPortal. Offering training is important to make users feel comfortable with the intranet. Engard and Park (2006) define training as "walking [users] through all of the new features" (23). This was not done during or immediately following the RefPortal's implementation. It was decided that minimal formal training was necessary. Instead, SharePoint administrators would work with individuals as the need arose. An overview of the RefPortal and its features was given at a monthly departmental meeting, and additional demonstrations have followed since the initial overview. While the administrators would have willingly provided more formalized, thorough training, a complex set of interdependent factors kept them from doing so.

Because the RefPortal was implemented in the fall of 2008—a notably busy time of the year for the Reference Department—SharePoint's administrators did not feel a rigid training program would be possible. Additionally, Cook Library's Reference Department is often used as a test case for new technologies because of their natural inquisitiveness, willingness to explore, and desire to provide feedback. It was assumed initially that individuals would bring forward questions as they arose. With the RefPortal, this was true in select cases but not universally. This was not because the new tool was rejected, as frequently happens with new technologies; the survey results actually indicated staff felt the portal had great potential and would be beneficial to the department. Instead, the lack of exploration had more to do with when they were required to begin exploring RefPortal. Because the RefPortal was primarily designed to be used while at the reference desk, staff did not have time to explore the new intranet in depth, much less add content or provide feedback, during the busy fall semester. This meant staff typically sought assistance only when they needed to perform a task that required using the RefPortal.

In retrospect, it would have been beneficial to introduce more staff to the RefPortal earlier in the implementation process when staff would have had more time to explore, add content, and provide feedback. Involving users during the testing phase of a new technology creates a greater sense of involvement with the new system and also provides a training opportunity. This involvement could have helped the RefPortal be more immediately successful. This would also increase the number of "expert" users who could then have helped train other users. SharePoint is a complex platform; while certain tasks are simple to perform, it is easy for the uninitiated user to get lost in the complexity of features available to them.

Training is an important part of the implementation of any new technology or service, but it is especially important to the success of an intranet. Without adequate training, users may not feel comfortable using the intranet, afraid that they will make an irreversible error. The success of the intranet is dependent on the contributions of its users. If nobody contributes, the information provided via the intranet becomes stagnant and outdated, leading users to other methods of communication. Adequate training should not be overlooked in the planning of an intranet.

Guaranteeing Success

As Galen Gruman (2008) suggested, a SharePoint intranet is best implemented by first focusing on those components that address specific needs. The four primary functions of the RefPortal are all well used because they support four basic needs identified by the department. Now that reference staff is familiar with the SharePoint interface, the platform can be expanded to encompass more functionality, addressing other departmental needs.

SharePoint also offers the ability to keep track of stats regarding site usage. This provides another method of analyzing the RefPortal's use beyond surveying reference staff. Based on individuals' usage statistics, a trophy called the "Reffy" is given out quarterly to one employee who has shown exemplary use of the RefPortal. Site usage statistics are essential for determining both who is using the portal and which areas of the portal are being used most frequently. Promoting exemplary use of the intranet is important, as it is common for staff to fall back on habitual methods for communicating and collaborating with other department members.

NEW DEVELOPMENTS AND FUTURE PLANS

The Reference Department's implementation of SharePoint has served as a model to other library departments and to the university. Towson's Office of Technology Services (OTS) makes SharePoint available to any department that would like a site, but use of SharePoint is not mandated by the university. Rather, implementation of SharePoint across the university has been a grassroots movement, spreading first through word of mouth and, more recently, through training sessions offered by the OTS. Many university committees now use SharePoint as a workspace for sharing documents and communicating between meetings.

As SharePoint is used by more committees and departments on campus, the ability for the Reference Department to communicate and collaborate with other segments of the university increases. Systems and services that affect multiple departments can be centrally managed more effectively. This is already true of the university's printing services. Multiple campus labs use the same pay-for-print service. Because the pay-for-print team uses SharePoint, printing issues can be reported in one place. The Reference Department's experience with and use of the SharePoint interface makes integration of new SharePoint sites quick and seamless. Running an intranet that integrates easily with other campus intranets has been one of the unforeseen benefits of SharePoint. Any library or library department planning to implement an intranet would be well-advised to share a common platform with other units with which frequent collaboration occurs.

The same grassroots implementation that has taken place across the university is also developing among other departments within the library. SharePoint sites for each department plus all library committees have been in place since the creation of the RefPortal but were not promoted or used by other library staff. Planning for expanded use of SharePoint has minimized the amount of work necessary, as other individuals, departments, and committees gain interest in using an intranet.

The library's Web Committee was an early adopter of SharePoint, largely because of the involvement of two reference librarians and the library technology coordinator on the committee. During a recent redesign of the library's Web site, the team was able to use SharePoint to map out a project timeline, share links to exemplary Web sites, post announcements and discussions, and assign tasks to particular individuals. Through assigned permissions, the redesign process was made available to any library staff who might be interested in the proceedings of the committee. This holds true for other areas of the library's intranet as well; every member of the library staff has—at a minimum—access to view other areas of the intranet. Very few cases exist where information in the portal is hidden because of the sensitivity of the content. This openness both reflects and enhances communication and collaboration within the library.

SharePoint offers numerous features that are not yet being used by the RefPortal. As is important with any technology solution, the technology should support the needs of the organization. SharePoint was identified as a product that could meet the immediate needs of the Reference Department, but it was also seen that SharePoint offered numerous features that could help address unidentified needs. As the RefPortal's designers gain more experience with the SharePoint environment and understand the tool's capabilities, new functions for the intranet become available, as do new tools for performing existing functions.

While the announcements Web part seemed like the intuitive tool to use for posting announcements in the RefPortal, it does not give users the ability to reply to the initial announcement. If follow-up actions are required, the only solution is to post a new announcement. This does not maintain any connection between the initial announcement and the follow-up. To solve this, the RefPortal is planning to migrate to SharePoint's Discussion

Thread component to manage the posting of announcements in the RefPortal. Discussion Threads allow replies to be posted to an initial announcement, fulfilling the department's needs more completely than before. This type of discovery can often only be made through trial and error. By implementing SharePoint within one department rather than initially deploying a library-wide implementation, the RefPortal designers have been able to learn and experiment with the SharePoint environment without requiring frequent changes in functionality to the intranet. The beta site has also enabled more experimentation with the SharePoint platform. As other departments gain interest in SharePoint, the designers of the RefPortal can more fully help them create a solution to fit their needs.

Several features of SharePoint remain unused or underused. The RefPortal uses the shared documents component to store the minutes from reference meetings and a few other key documents. Files in the shared documents area can be modified by several individuals, and SharePoint retains previous versions for reference. This is a useful yet sparsely used feature of the RefPortal. This component of SharePoint is expected to be used more, as new documents are created by the department. As use of the shared documents space increases, a plan for organizing, editing, and retrieving documents will need to be developed.

The RefPortal also offers the opportunity to share information of professional interest among members of the library staff. A "Links and Feeds" page exists for this purpose, offering RSS feeds for several relevant blogs and links to Web sites of professional interest (see Figure 5). This portion of the portal does not receive heavy use yet. Most staff wishing to share Web links and other information related to librarianship still rely on e-mail. Promotion

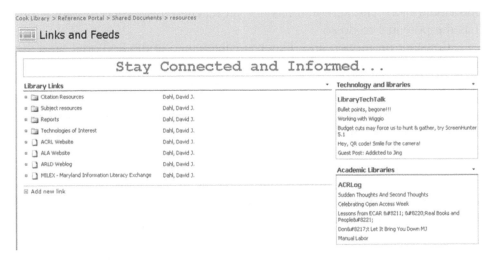

FIGURE 5 Links and Feeds page with links to blogs and professional Web sites.

and training could help make this a more used tool. E-mail has become the default communication tool for most organizations; changing this habit to a new communication method takes constant and continued attention. The benefits to using an intranet rather than e-mail are that the information is centralized, preserved, and searchable, and individuals will no longer need to make decisions on whether they need to keep an e-mail containing a Web link, where to store the information, or with whom to share it.

Other SharePoint components remain unexplored but could be of use in the RefPortal, including blogs, calendars, and task lists. Determining uses for these components will take place concurrently with continued evaluation of the efficiency and effectiveness of the current SharePoint implementation. SharePoint's survey tool will continue to be a useful assessment tool, as will less formal avenues of assessment. As use of SharePoint expands from the RefPortal to a wider library intranet, new avenues of communication will open. Future evaluation and refinement of the library's workflows will need to include SharePoint.

CONCLUSION

Intranets often suffer from a "catch 22." Users will not post content in an intranet because they are unsure whether others will see it; meanwhile, users will not access the intranet because information is not being posted there. Often, communications will still be duplicated in e-mails or other forms of communication. Ultimately, the goal of the intranet should be to provide one-stop access to all departmental communication and knowledge. When this occurs, the intranet becomes a widely used, necessary tool for each individual's job. The RefPortal has not yet reached this level of ubiquity, but has the potential to do so.

Constant promotion and diligent maintenance of the RefPortal (and the rest of the library's intranet) is necessary to continue or even increase its role in the library's communication and collaboration efforts. The most important factor to the success of any intranet is trust (Wisniewski 2006). Users must trust the intranet to fulfill their communication and information-seeking needs. If it is not trusted, it becomes just one more thing to check—or to forget to check.

While SharePoint has proven to be a good intranet solution for Cook Library's Reference Department, other options may be more appropriate to other libraries and library departments. A thorough needs assessment should be conducted, and a solution should be sought that fulfills those needs. Adequate training should be included in the intranet's implementation plan, and feedback should be sought to evaluate whether the intranet is meeting the users' needs.

SharePoint is an easily configured intranet solution that provides extensive options for customizing and extending its functionality. The basic SharePoint components can be customized to serve several different purposes, and the resulting Web parts can be reused in multiple locations to make information sharing easier. Paired with Microsoft Office, SharePoint has become an incredibly useful system for document management and collaboration, allowing the department to produce searchable documents. The inclusion of Web 2.0 features, like blogs and wikis, reflects the changing nature of intranets, making content more accessible for all users. SharePoint is a vital tool for the Cook Library Reference Department and will only grow in importance as its use expands throughout the library and the university.

REFERENCES

Bejune, Matthew M. 2007. Wikis in libraries. *Information Technology and Libraries* 26(3): 26–38.

Benzing, Matthew M. 1998. Intranets for the CD-ROM librarian. *Computers in Libraries* 18(9): 54–57.

Dworak, Ellie, and Keven Jeffery. 2009. Wiki to the rescue: Creating a more dynamic intranet. *Library Hi Tech* 27(3): 403–410.

Engard, Nicole C., and RayAna M. Park. 2006. Intranet 2.0: Fostering collaboration. *Online* 30(3): 16–23.

Gruman, Galen. 2008. SharePoint with a little bit of everything. *CIO* 21(8): 19–23.

Herrera, Kevin. 2008. From static files to collaborative workspace with SharePoint. *Library Hi Tech* 26(1): 80–94.

Holtz, Shel. 2008. Bring your intranet into the 21st century. *Communication World* 25(1, January): 14–18.

McIntyre, Alison, and Janette Nicolle. 2008. Biblioblogging: Blogs for library communication. *The Electronic Library* 26(5): 683–694.

Michel, Roberto. 2008. Office goes server-side: Microsoft's blending of Office with SharePoint begets enterprise collaboration platform. *Manufacturing Business Technology* 26(3): 40–42.

Sheehan, Kate. 2009. Creating open source conversation. *Computers in Libraries* 29(2): 8–11.

van Rooij, Shahron Williams. 2007. Perceptions of open source versus commercial software: Is higher education still on the fence? *Journal of Research on Technology in Education* 39(4): 433–453.

Welsh, Anne. 2007. Internal wikis for procedures and training. *Online* 31(6): 26–29.

Wisniewski, Jeff. 2006. Getting a handle on content. *Online* 30(2): 52–54.

APPENDIX A: JANUARY 2009 REFPORTAL USABILITY AND SATISFACTION SURVEY

1. Where do you use the Reference Portal? (select all that apply)

    Home   Office   Reference Desk   Other_____

2. How often do you use the following features of the Reference Portal? (Answers: Monthly, Weekly, Daily, Never)

    Announcements   Discussion Forum   Issue Tracking
    Links and Feeds page   Reference Wiki   Shared Documents
    StatsTracker

3. Which feature of the Reference Portal do you like the most? (choose one)

    Announcements   Discussion Forum   Issue Tracking
    Links and Feeds page   Reference Wiki   Shared Documents
    StatsTracker

4. Which feature of the Reference Portal do you like the least? (choose one)

    Announcements   Discussion Forum   Issue Tracking
    Links and Feeds page   Reference Wiki   Shared Documents
    StatsTracker

5. Please rate the importance of the features of the Reference Portal. (1 = Not Important, 5 = Extremely Important)

    Announcements   Discussion Forum   Issue Tracking
    Links and Feeds page   Reference Wiki   Shared Documents
    StatsTracker

6. Please select your level of agreeance with the following statements. (1 = strongly disagree, 5 = strongly agree)

    I am aware of everything I can do with the Reference Portal.
    I use all of the features available to me in the Reference Portal.
    I feel comfortable using the features of the Reference Portal.
    I have had sufficient training for using the Reference Portal.
    The Reference Portal improves staff communication.
    I can find useful information in the Reference Portal.

7. Please rate the Reference Portal (1–5) according to the following criteria.

    Aesthetics   Ease of use   Efficiency   Navigation   Usefulness

8. Please provide any additional comments or suggestions below.

A Point to Share: Streamlining Access Services Workflow Through Online Collaboration, Communication, and Storage with Microsoft SharePoint

JENNIFER DIFFIN, FANUEL CHIROMBO, DENNIS NANGLE, and MARK DE JONG

Information and Library Services, University of Maryland, Adelphi, Maryland, USA

This article explains how the document management team (circulation and interlibrary loan) at the University of Maryland University College implemented Microsoft's SharePoint product to create a central hub for online collaboration, communication, and storage. Enhancing the team's efficiency, organization, and cooperation was the primary goal. Although the group is already highly effective, it is always interested in making further improvements. Document Management consists of three technicians and two professionals, and this small staff is responsible for providing services to 86,000 students plus faculty and staff at a distance education-focused institution. The team's previously adopted tools to improve internal operations had been adequate but not optimal. Also, a long-standing and overarching concern about the potential loss of some or all of the document management knowledge base existed. These reasons prompted the team to carefully examine SharePoint as a prospective tool. It was hoped that this early scrutiny would prove beneficial in the long run by avoiding a repeat of earlier technology implementations' shortcomings. The group quickly realized the software would not be a cure-all but felt the prospects were good that it would be useful and dependable. SharePoint was fully implemented with great success because of the team's careful consideration of collaboration, communication, and storage needs.

Internal communication, workflows, and teamwork can often be greatly improved through the intelligent application of appropriate technologies. However, libraries sometimes ignore or misapply information technology, which often negatively affects staff and patrons. As a predominantly distance education campus serving a global population, the University of Maryland University College (UMUC) relies heavily on information technology to meet student, faculty, and staff needs. From its modest beginnings in 1947, UMUC has grown to more than 86,000 students in more than twenty countries (University of Maryland University College 2009). Information and Library Services (ILS) at UMUC has depended on savvy staff and technological solutions out of necessity in order to provide library services to UMUC's students, faculty, and staff worldwide.

HISTORY/BACKGROUND

ILS's document management (DM) team, which provides circulation and interlibrary loan services, recognized workflow issues beginning in 2005. Over the previous few years, ILS had grown from a handful of staff to more than two dozen librarians and technicians. This rapid growth created lapses in knowledge, documentation, and information-sharing behavior, as individual responsibilities changed and new services were developed. Originally, the DM team used five print binders as house training manuals and troubleshooting guides. These were fed by centrally stored digital documents held on a shared network drive. During the growth period, updates to these binders became ad hoc. No single binder contained the most current or most accurate information. In fact, there was a good chance that one could uncover multiple solutions to one problem. Further complicating this, the shared network drive, which was created to hold the most authoritative versions of all documentation, suffered from the staff increases as well. Nearly all information was scattered in personal folders, current documents could not be differentiated from the outdated ones, and documentation was poorly labeled. This made it virtually impossible to locate the precise document needed. Furthermore, the network drive supported all of ILS, not just the DM team, making it more difficult to quickly locate needed documentation and compromising team productivity. The DM team did make a concerted effort to customize a portion of the network drive. The team created new folders specifically for circulation and ILL, and it moved a great deal of relevant documentation into them. Although it became a convenient location to place documents the team needed to access, no set standards were followed. Staff members were unaware of changes to documents, thereby rendering the information inconsistent and unreliable. At this point, the team decided that an entirely new solution was required.

The DM team's first attempt to grow beyond the network-drive-and-binders arrangement involved a Web-based manual. It was believed all staff would be able to access information using a single, easy-to-update online source. However, the site remained unconnected to the Internet because of unresolved security issues, such as password protection and privacy concerns. After one year, the Web concept was determined not to be a complete solution. The team then developed a wiki as a kind of "Band-Aid," with the understanding that this was not a robust solution; the wiki was on a test server that was neither supported nor maintained by the university's IT department. Also, as is true of wikis, it could not support critical spreadsheet and word processing documents.

After taking stock of the previous knowledge management systems, the DM team identified three overarching problems: disparate communication, collaboration, and storage. This is not to say that the team was entirely lacking in collaboration or effective communication. Neither does it imply that knowledge storage was completely haphazard. The team then realized the key to moving forward successfully was to discover and implement a system with one centralized location, which would eliminate redundancy and knowledge gaps and encourage information sharing among DM staff.

LOOKING FOR A STREAMLINED SOLUTION

As a first step, the team decided to strategically review DM's knowledge management needs in light of its roles and duties. Within ILS, the DM team is one of the front-line service points for patrons. Thus, staff must be accurately informed of policy and procedure changes in DM and ILS. They also need to be able to quickly access information to provide timely and accurate responses to patron inquiries. Service delays and misinformation could potentially cause unacceptable patron inconveniences because of UMUC's largely virtual environment.

As a result of this review, the team implemented a universal organization standard based on Anne Thompson's "Standard Naming Conventions for Electronic Records" (2005). This was then used to store documents, which, in turn, made locating and saving documents more efficient and reliable. After fully assessing the problem, the team recognized that beyond possessing a common standard, they needed a regularly maintained and centralized knowledge base.

In 2008, the team evaluated several products that might provide a more robust solution. One tool DM evaluated was Microsoft SharePoint 2007 (http://sharepoint.microsoft.com/product/Pages/default.aspx), because it was already installed at the university and centrally managed by the university's IT department. SharePoint is a centralized platform for storage and communication that combines several Web 2.0 technologies with traditional digital document storage to facilitate a consolidated workflow. The team was initially impressed with the potential of SharePoint because it integrates many technologies that the team already used in one central location. The team had a wiki, a calendaring system, and a document storage system, but these were stand-alone systems. SharePoint puts all these and more in one integrated application. After evaluating all the pros and cons of Share-Point, the DM team determined that by implementing SharePoint, they could significantly improve their workflows.

IMPLEMENTING A NEW SOLUTION

In the initial implementation phase, the team began moving documentation from several decentralized channels into SharePoint. During this pilot phase, it became apparent that the problems encountered in previous systems might be duplicated in SharePoint if standards were not developed. Thus, the team created a best practices document to provide guidelines on naming conventions, document retention, and appropriate applications of the SharePoint tools. This approach ensured that the migrated information was organized logically to enhance the usability of SharePoint's features, such as the wiki and document library.

Because of some staff turnover, the move to SharePoint began slowly. Once the migration was underway, it became evident that SharePoint offers many streamlining features that were previously not available to the DM team. Remote accessibility through a Virtual Private Network (VPN) allows staff to log in from home if needed. It has a built-in wiki and document library that can be used as a knowledge base. Beyond the knowledge base capabilities, SharePoint also allows for collaboration and communication to come together in one place. SharePoint's customizable homepage allows several notifications and features to be displayed as soon as the user logs in (see Figure 1). Automatic e-mail alerts notify staff when changes are made to any SharePoint site section, including documents, the wiki, etc. Staff can choose to receive alerts immediately so they are instantly aware of issues and can deal with them right away. The e-mail alerts make a huge impact on keeping staff current and help build a more collaborative team.

When a document was edited on the shared drive, it was often saved as a different version under a new name. It quickly became difficult to tell which document was the official, current version. The SharePoint version history control in the wiki and document library allows staff to update documents and wiki pages without fear of losing previous versions. Only one version of each document (the most current) is visible, while all previous versions

FIGURE 1 The DM SharePoint homepage displays a Twitter feed, schedules, etc.

are hidden but still available. This function simplifies organization, saves staff time, and eliminates confusion by making it easy to identify the correct version. Team members have also been able to save time editing documents by mapping SharePoint as a network drive on their computers. Documents and wiki pages can be saved and edited directly through their PC's "My Network Places" rather than by accessing the SharePoint site itself (see Figure 2).

COLLABORATION

Many of SharePoint's features had the potential to facilitate collaboration from within a centralized hub. The team held several meetings to discuss how to thoughtfully approach the wiki in SharePoint, which resulted in a project timeline, wiki table of contents, style guide, and reference manual for developing wiki pages. The team began framing the wiki's structure by using the relevant content from the previous wiki. Initially, two separate wikis existed in SharePoint: one for circulation processes and another for ILL duties. While the team worked on developing the structure, it became apparent that two wikis were inefficient and unnecessary, and the team restructured the content under the categorical umbrella of "Document Management." Under this approach, categories like "Contacts," "Passwords," and "Shipping" contained all information for both circulation and ILL. Once the structure was complete, the three library technicians began to share the wiki migration project with the library's six part-time student workers.

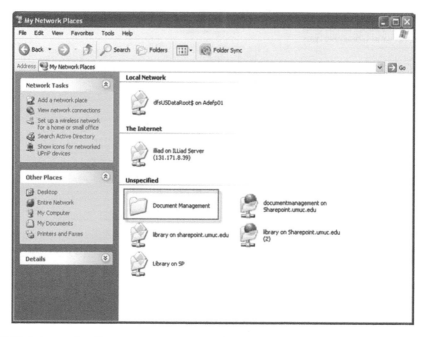

FIGURE 2 Once the SharePoint site is mapped, users can access and save items through their PCs.

To prepare and train these new contributors, the team created a Word document that outlined how the wiki pages were to be structured, whether a student or full-time employee should complete the task, and which sections were completed. Once the expectations were clear, the team introduced the student workers to a special wiki page that explained how to properly create and design individual wiki pages. Additionally, a style guide allowed the wiki to look cohesive and uniform among the several hands involved in its creation.

As the team was navigating the previous Web-based wiki, they realized that pages were text-heavy and impeded staff from easily referencing a particular process or policy. One way the team solved this problem was to rely on visual examples via screenshots. However, more careful planning was required to successfully integrate this visual element into the wiki. The team, therefore, created a "Wiki Screenshots" photo library in SharePoint, which acts much like the document library feature but provides more support for certain photo-hosting functions. With 156 screenshots in use in 159 wiki pages, it was essential that the team establish standards. For screenshot files, the team continued to use Thompson's conventions. DM decided to structure the photo library directory to mirror the wiki layout (see Figure 3).

Since the screenshot process is a relatively tedious one, the team instructed all wiki page developers to write the text first, with placeholders indicating where a screenshot should be placed. After the text was completed,

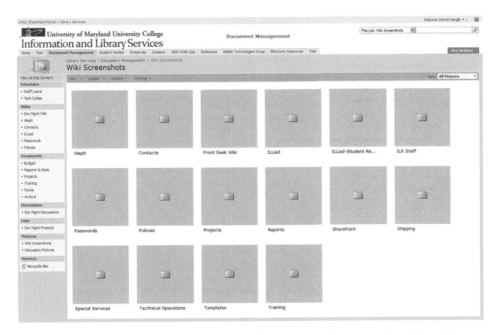

FIGURE 3 The "Wiki Screenshots" photo library mirrors the categories of the wiki.

the page creator was responsible for taking and inserting the corresponding screenshots. To facilitate uniformity, a separate instructional page was created that could be referenced to learn how to create screenshots using three different tools. Because of the diverse resources within the library, several screenshot methods had to be explored and documented. By using standards to supplement SharePoint's features, staff could easily contribute to the wiki implementation project.

Extending beyond creating standards and documentation, the team also took advantage of several SharePoint features to integrate fearless collaboration with seamless communication. The team was able to put its trust in several contributors, since SharePoint allows them to revert to previous versions of wiki pages in the event a page creator makes an error. Any changes a page creator makes are clearly color coded, so if a team member needs to make corrections, there is no need to meticulously read through the previous version (see Figure 4). Also, whenever a staff member makes a change to a wiki page, individuals receive an e-mail alert. Any member of the library can subscribe to specific alerts. This feature solves a major issue the team had with the previous wiki; those referring to the wiki were mistrustful of the content since they could not necessarily rely on the information's validity.

Finally, the team felt more secure having the wiki on the SharePoint server, which is housed in and supported by the university's IT department and is backed up daily. The previous wiki was housed on a spare computer in an office instead of on an official server with nightly backups. Also, this

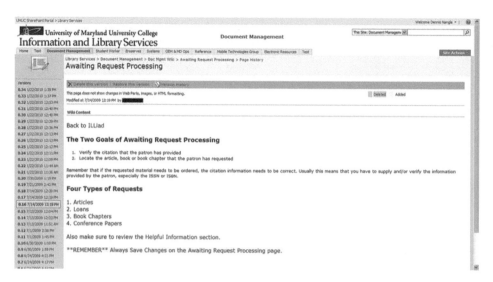

FIGURE 4 An example of the version history feature in a wiki context.

computer was housed neither within the library nor in IT; therefore, DM had little control over it, and it was neither supported nor maintained by IT. The computer was dated and had been known to occasionally crash, making the DM team nervous about losing data that would be difficult to replicate without any backups.

COMMUNICATION

One of the quick resolutions to the communication issue was the implementation of various calendars. The SharePoint calendar system is immediately usable because of its intuitiveness, yet it serves a powerful function. The DM team set up their calendars to schedule and streamline workflow for the technicians and student workers. The team created three primary calendars: "Tech Duty Schedule," "Student Worker Schedule," and "Staff Leave Schedule." The three technicians ensured rotation of their responsibilities by creating a monthly schedule of their daily tasks and adding it on the Tech Duty schedule in SharePoint (see Figure 5).

The DM team's library associate is responsible for creating the student worker schedule that displays the student workers' hourly activities. The library associate uses this schedule as a quick reference tool when preparing information for student payroll. The entire library staff uses the schedule to identify individual students who can help with certain tasks on a particular day. The student workers refer to their calendar to coordinate their work activities.

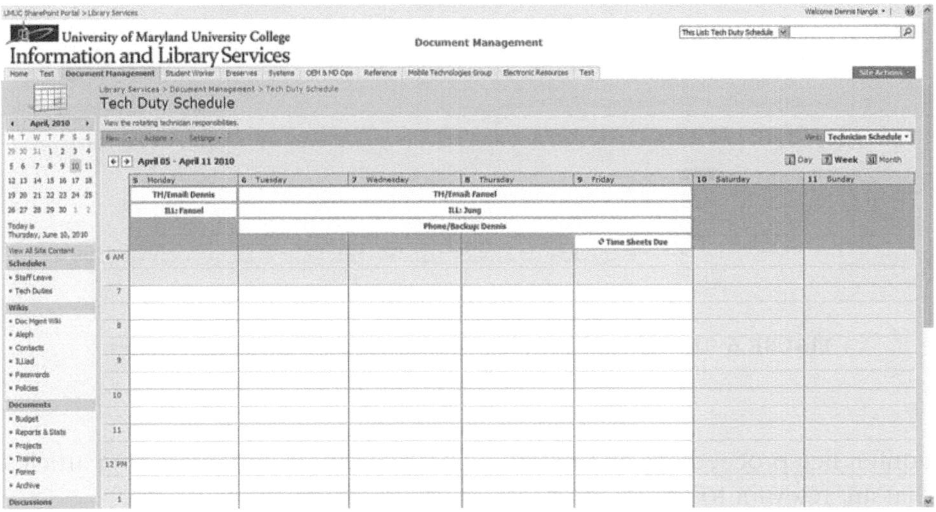

FIGURE 5 Document Management's "Tech Duty Schedule."

Individual team members are responsible for recording their absence from work on the staff leave schedule. The information recorded on this schedule ranges from a few hours of absence to leave days. The team members record the reasons for absence, for example, arriving late or leaving early. The leave calendar also keeps a record of staff working outside their normally scheduled hours.

Both library management and team members find the leave calendar to be a handy reference point when completing timesheets. Since every team member is aware of what the others are doing, it is also a simple and effective way to coordinate work activities. Management also refers to the schedules when following up on tasks or when identifying team members who could help with other tasks. Other library departments, like the reference team, also rely on the tech duty schedule when routing telephone and e-mail inquiries that need DM technicians' attention. Beyond coordination, the calendar is an important communication tool for team members. E-mail alerts are received when changes are made to help staff prepare their work accordingly.

The DM team set up a discussion board on their SharePoint site to facilitate and effectively manage communication. Here, team members discuss work-related topics by posting queries, comments, and questions and by responding to postings. The team uses the discussion board to build consensus on issues that require group decision making. Team members can respond to discussions while working on other tasks at their desks, eliminating the need for time-consuming meetings. The team is able to permanently store discussions so they are quickly referenced and easy to access. The team also created an announcements section on SharePoint to post essential information for professional development. Team members share information on

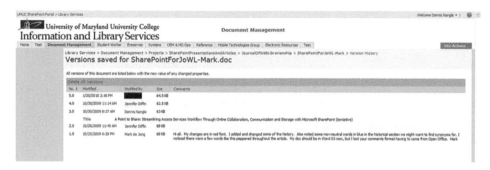

FIGURE 6 The version history view for SharePoint's document libraries.

conference proceedings and external library partners and interesting articles that are relevant to library work.

STORAGE

In preparation for the transition into SharePoint, the DM team carefully approached the issue of document storage. As mentioned above, the team had already used Thompson's (2005) naming conventions to reorganize the existing files. However, DM also carefully assessed the utility of their existing documents: which files were still relevant and which documents could serve a more effective purpose by being reformatted as a wiki page. A total of 1,167 reports, forms, records, and other documents remained after this weeding process was complete. Fortunately, the actual act of uploading the documents to SharePoint was the simplest part of the process. It took two part-time student workers only two days to complete the project.

The DM team now creates, stores, and shares files using the Share-Point document library. The team uses this site to store various file types, such as Microsoft Word, PowerPoint, and Excel (http://office.microsoft.com/) and Adobe Acrobat (http://www.adobe.com/products/acrobat/). Every team member can open and edit these files. SharePoint's version history allows team members to track the original document before changes were made (see Figure 6). This is a major advantage over the shared network drive because the drive did not provide a platform to track changes made to a saved document. The team now finds files quickly and easily with SharePoint's search feature.

While the concept of document storage is often viewed as an inorganic system, infusing it with SharePoint's Web-based features has reinvigorated the process. Since all items uploaded to SharePoint are automatically assigned a unique URL, disseminating a document is as easy as copying, pasting, and sending a URL. The team often writes Sticky Notes and announcements that refer to a specific document, and the writer can include the link to the document within the post.

LESSONS LEARNED

While the transition to SharePoint as a DM system has generally been very beneficial in streamlining the DM team's workflow, the process was not without its obstacles. At the time, DM's university IT liaison for SharePoint-related questions also had many other higher priority duties; therefore, he was sometimes unavailable to immediately address questions. However, he was always willing to work with the team when his schedule permitted. Also, some SharePoint functionality is restricted by the University's current versions of Microsoft Exchange Server (http://technet.microsoft.com/en-us/library/bb123872(EXCHG.65).aspx) and Windows Server Active Directory (http://www.microsoft.com/windowsserver2003/technologies/directory/activedirectory/default.mspx).

Although the university is using Microsoft SharePoint Server Services 2007, it uses the 2003 versions of Microsoft Office and Exchange Server. This limits the full capabilities of SharePoint 2007. Each time staff members open documents from SharePoint, it requires them to log in again. The different server versions prohibit synchronization capabilities between the SharePoint and Microsoft Outlook calendars. This requires users to manually synchronize and update calendars between Outlook and SharePoint. These compatibility problems may also be responsible for some e-mail alert irregularities. Some staff have experienced inconsistency in receiving alerts via e-mail in addition to receiving them in a strange format. Fortunately, these issues will be resolved in the near future when the university upgrades to Exchange Server 2007 and Microsoft Office 2007.

Also, as a Microsoft product, SharePoint works best in Microsoft's Internet Explorer (http://www.microsoft.com/windows/internet-explorer/). Some products the library uses, such as Springshare's LibGuides (http://www.springshare.com/libguides/), work better in Mozilla Firefox (http://www.mozilla.com/en-US/firefox/ie.html), which many staff members prefer. Staff must remember to switch to Internet Explorer when working in SharePoint to fully use its functions.

While the version history for documents is superior to what the team was using before the move to SharePoint, only one person being able to edit a document at a time is a limitation to some group projects. If someone has a document "checked out," that document is essentially locked, except for a view-only version, until it is once again "checked in." If the person forgets to check in the document, there is no known way to override the check out.

The minimal amount of SharePoint documentation and training provided to the team led them to develop their own instructions and best practices.

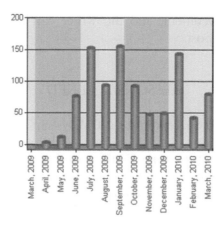

FIGURE 7 Usage statistics for Document Management's site, representing average site request per day.

This documentation was often based on trial and error as the team developed its SharePoint site. The lessons learned are being passed on to other teams in the library who are interested in using a SharePoint site of their own.

CONCLUSION

Overall, SharePoint has proven useful to DM's communication and team-work objectives. The document version history, wiki, calendar, discussion board, announcements, and alerts features have all been a boon to the team. Average site visits to SharePoint have increased from about ten per day in May 2009 to 140 in January 2010 (see Figure 7). Of course, critical thinking prior to and during implementation was important to the process. Without the human element and smart interventions, SharePoint may not have been used to its full potential; it is a powerful tool, yet it requires a thoughtful approach.

Based on the success of the implementation, a DM technician was invited to present to the entire library staff on how the team used SharePoint for communication, collaboration, and document storage. This sparked the interest of several additional library teams: the electronic reserves team is creating their first online manual using SharePoint; the digital resources librarian is considering using it for knowledge management; and finally, the systems team has begun to use SharePoint for a knowledge base and document storage. The university's IT department has praised DM's early adoption of and success with SharePoint within UMUC and expressed interest in possibly using it as a model for other departments.

Although the university's IT department still retains the highest level of control, the team has a significant amount of control over the customization of SharePoint within their site. While it is relatively easy to jump in and start using some basic SharePoint features, the number of features, capabilities, and customizations available in the product can be overwhelming for hopeful adopters. Nonetheless, this should not be a deterrent since DM still continues to learn about new SharePoint possibilities as use of the product increases.

REFERENCES

Thompson, Anne. 2005. Standard naming conventions for electronic records. http://www.sfu.ca/archives2/rm/rm_fundamentals/07UKFileNamingConventions.pdf (accessed August 1, 2009).

University of Maryland University College. Office of Institutional Planning, Research and Accountability. 2009. UMUC quick facts. http://www.umuc.edu/ip/quickfacts.shtml (accessed February 1, 2010).

Intranet 2.0 from a Project Management Perspective

PAUL A. SHARPE

University of Missouri, St. Louis, St. Louis, Missouri, USA

RACHEL E. VACEK

University of Houston Libraries, Houston, Texas, USA

Library intranets require flexibility and efficiency and enhance the internal communication and collaborative nature of creating and organizing the institution's information. At the University of Houston Libraries, the focus was on public services, so little attention was given to the intranet—the tool every department relied on for quick access to their content. Text-heavy, static Web pages with poor organization and outdated information made the site unusable. In 2008, the University of Houston Libraries assembled a team to begin the considerable task of redesigning the intranet with Drupal, a popular open source content management system that would allow for interactive information sharing, user-centered design, and new ways of collaboration. This article outlines on the overall project management of the intranet redesign process, including methods used for collecting staff feedback, evaluating existing and potential content, creating a new information architecture focused on departments and committees, establishing new internal communication channels, creating staff enthusiasm and buy-in, and training the entire library staff.

The advent of Web 2.0 and its applications in the realm of library services has brought with it a flurry of exciting projects, followed by many scholarly works documenting their progress. Library Web and IT professionals everywhere have been eagerly exploring the wild frontier of open source development and integrating early Web 2.0 tools such as blogs, RSS feeds, and wikis. These tools aid in sharing information, which is an essential part of any management strategy. While the concept of an intranet predates these tools and concepts, it is still one of the most practical technological needs libraries have today. An intranet provides a focal point for internal communication and collaboration. Many libraries have been moving their intranet sites away from the traditional HTML design and toward content management systems (CMSs) that facilitate the major concepts of Web 2.0: interactive information sharing, interoperability, user-centered design, and collaboration.

Much of the literature in this area remains focused on the choice and/or benefits of a particular CMS or the benefits of migrating to a more dynamic, easier-to-maintain system. There is little focus on how the projects were implemented and shepherded to fruition. It is all too easy to be excited by newly available tools and an aesthetically pleasing intranet site. However, the necessity for careful planning cannot be underestimated. For this reason, during the design and implementation of the University of Houston (UH) Libraries' new intranet site, special consideration was given to how the project was managed.

The UH Libraries' intranet, as it existed prior to redesign (see Figure 1), consisted of primarily static HTML pages; the collective knowledge, tools,

FIGURE 1 UH Libraries' old intranet, built on static HTML pages.

forms, and memories of a large academic library were relegated to a single page of hyperlinks. There was no global navigation, and search functionality was faulty at best. Pages were maintained by anyone in the library, which compromised the control of information organization, currency, and format. Those unfamiliar with HTML tended to turn Microsoft Word documents into Web pages, bypassing the intranet's intended template and style sheet. In addition, much of the information was outdated. Representation was inconsistent; not every department and committee had an intranet presence. Of those that did, many had great depths of information and archives, sometimes more than was necessary for a functional communication tool. Staff members within the library also urgently needed easier access to forms, policies, procedures, meeting minutes, and library news in general. As can be imagined, this intranet was a relic, an embarrassment for any self-respecting Web developer. This was the perfect jumping-off point for a redesign project.

There were already many new external tools and services being used within the UH Libraries, including blogs and wikis. Library users could tag and comment on items within the blogs and the catalog. Yet these tools existed apart from and outside the intranet. It made sense that some of these same functions should be integrated internally as well. With the beginnings of a project in mind, it became clear that determining the process would be as pivotal as identifying the right technology. It is from this perspective that the importance of effective project management as it applies to the intranet redesign process is asserted.

LITERATURE REVIEW

As previously mentioned, there is very little focus on overall project management when it comes to Web and technology projects, particularly within the library realm. Perhaps the only directly applicable model comes from Darlene Fichter (2001), who laid out the process from start to finish. Her discussion of learning the lessons of first-generation intranets was certainly appropriate for its time, and it resonated with the past experiences of the authors. However, it lacks the currency and perspective of post-Web 2.0 achievements that inform today's process.

Lori Wamsley (2009) provided a current exploration of library staff management, which applies to this project on certain levels. Her article illustrated how to focus on maintaining engagement and buy-in with staff, which was a key to the redesign process of UH's project. The general nature of Wamsley's article provided an overall framework yet lacked the technological focus needed at UH. An even more granular approach to planning the necessary steps is presented by Lisa German (2009) in her take on technical services projects at Penn State. Her concept of a project charter, laying out all of the key components of a specific project, translates quite well into the charge from library administration for UH's project. It also mirrors the plan set forth by the chair of the task force, providing a road map by which to measure the project's success.

Martin White (2007) presented a succinct argument that directly addressed the topic at hand. His writing concurred with the Wamsley approach of bringing together all stakeholders in the design process, adding that this direction goes beyond being merely operational and is, in fact, a strategic approach. White asserted content guardianship over ownership, distributing the responsibility across the organization.

In their book *Intranets for Info Pros*, Mary Lee Kennedy and Jane Dysart (2007) covered more of the organizational and informational aspects of intranets rather than focusing on the technological approaches to building and managing it. Much of the information, which comes from several experts in the field, includes implementation, creating and organizing information, content management, information architecture, user design, and even intranet search. Throughout the book, they emphasized that strategic planning and the organization of information is crucial, because the best technology and prettiest designs cannot help with usability or with getting people to use an intranet. Rather than being library-specific, the book is directed more broadly toward information professionals in general. However, it is a valuable resource for helping libraries think strategically about their intranets.

Each of these works touches upon an aspect of the project at hand without being a direct corollary. While all have their merits, none provided both currency and specificity for the current task. For purposes of this discussion, the hope is to present a combination of the best ideas within these works and how they lend themselves to the success of this or any other technology project.

PROJECT PROLOGUE

In early 2008, the UH Libraries' intranet was in a dismal state. When the Web Services coordinator approached library administration with a proposal to redesign the intranet, it was met with much enthusiasm. Creating buy-in from library staff was almost effortless, yet the fear of change threatened the success of the project. In addition, multiple communication methods, often thought to provide redundancy, were actually overloading the daily habits of the library staff. The answer would come from consolidating information delivery into a single portal. A newly designed intranet could serve that purpose. But in order for a new intranet to be successful and eliminate confusion, library staff members needed to alter the ways they received and shared information. Managing the implementation of a new intranet meant focusing on two major goals: redesigning the heavily used but antiquated intranet site and facilitating a paradigm shift in the way the UH Libraries approached internal communication.

A couple of key decisions were made at the onset. The first was having a formal charge. While formality is not necessary in every process, having clearly defined goals definitely eases the transition. Awareness of expectations is critical in project management, regardless of the scope of the undertaking. Another decision made early on was establishing a strict and accelerated timeline because of a general malaise associated with lengthy projects within the libraries. The project was set to start in June 2008, with the new intranet going live in January 2009 and total project completion by June 2009. The old intranet would remain available until June 2009, allowing time for the migration and creation of information as well as redundancy during the transition.

To keep the project on time and on target, it was determined ahead of time that the CMS for the new intranet would be Drupal (http://drupal.org/). The benefits of using open source software include generally low overhead and customizability. Drupal is a widely used CMS that provides the flexible architecture and modular design necessary for various groups to present their information in a meaningful way. With the appropriate modules installed, a Drupal-based intranet could support a variety of content types. As library staff members created and incorporated more content, taxonomies and folksonomies could develop to aid in organizing the overall information architecture of the site (Fichter 2006). Everyone within the organization would have the ability to create and edit any page without knowledge of HTML, thus promoting collaboration in the building of Web pages throughout the site.

With the charge, a proposed timeline, and a recommended CMS in hand, the next step was to convene a task force. The UH Libraries sought a balance between the technical expertise required for redesign and the broad engagement of the organization needed to propel the process forward. Consistent with the anecdotal evidence and general consensus, it was determined that a representational team would be assembled to assess the libraries' broader needs. The task force was made up of a mix of librarians and staff from the following areas: Web services, instruction, administration, human resources, acquisitions, access services, liaison services, and branch libraries.

The nine members of the Intranet Redesign Task Force were charged with interviewing their respective departments and soliciting feedback from all key stakeholders. The task force would then reconvene, with each member representing the needs and views unique to their areas of the library. The libraries' Web Services coordinator would serve as chair, working as a liaison between the decision-making body of the task force and the Web Services department. Web Services would then make the necessary changes and modifications to the site.

A project presence was established within Basecamp (http://base camphq.com/) to provide a centralized means of communication. By organizing through project management software, all members of the committee were allowed access to documents, e-mail, survey results, and any other pertinent materials at any time. In addition, such software provided a built-in means of adhering to the established timeline.

THE PROJECT

From the initial discussions of the group as a whole, three central questions were brought to the forefront. Why do users go to the intranet now? Why might they go in the future? From the point of view of each department and committee, what information needs to be communicated to library staff throughout the organization? To capture the thoughts of intranet end users, the task force felt it was important to first research the needs of library staff by developing a short online survey using SurveyMonkey (http://www.surveymonkey.com/). The questionnaire (see Appendix A) sought to capture basic usage statistics and the current and potential uses for the intranet. The survey also served as both an introduction to some newer terms and an informal gauge of awareness of current and emerging trends in Web communication. In all, 29 completed surveys were received, achieving a 21 percent response rate among UH Libraries staff members.

Task force members were given time to conduct the necessary interviews within their areas of the organization. These sessions also became an informal method of explaining the possibilities of a new intranet site. Resistance to change is normal within a large organization; however, by educating the staff on what might be achieved through a retooled intranet, a number of new techniques were envisioned and subsequently developed. The task force reconvened with a list of needs and new ideas for improving workflow.

Besides generating new ideas from departmental conversations, task force members were also assigned to review the current intranet site. The group was asked to identify content that belonged to a specific department, committee, or other entity within the organization. Additionally, members identified outdated or obsolete material. The group then determined if these items retained any historic value and whether they should be archived. Items deemed to be without any value were not migrated to the new intranet site.

Evaluating content from the old intranet proved daunting but not impossible. Items identified as worthless by some were important to others. The task was to sort the sacred cows from the orphaned and dead links. A mixture of departmental policies, committee meeting minutes, LibQUAL+ results, and photos from past library events lived within the structure of the old intranet. Members of the task force worked closely with each department to identify homes for both old and new content inside the presumed architecture of the future site.

Simultaneously, Web Services was able to draw many conclusions from the data collected in the departmental interviews. The development of wireframes began in fall 2008. A rapid cycle of design, feedback, and redesign developed between the task force and Web Services. The process of honing and fine-tuning the finished product continued through a short series of online prototypes. In this fashion, the new site began to take shape and was slowly brought online one department at a time in January 2009. The new intranet was almost empty when it was shown to the public; only the underlying structure of the main pages, menus, and taxonomies had been created. For some departments, beginning with a blank slate would have been intimidating. Departments that had recently revamped their old intranet pages and had content ready to migrate to the Drupal site were chosen to go first; departments that had their content organized and ready for the new site were close to follow. By the time the remaining departments began using their intranet space, they could look to the pages of the early adopters to generate ideas and plan the organization of their content and navigation.

Cataloging and Metadata Services was the first department to have its content ready. It became the perfect candidate to test the new environment and the model for others to follow. Administration, Reference & Instructional Services, and Human Resources soon followed. After those departments were settled into their new space, the task force stopped to assess the successes and challenges thus far, adjusting the implementation process as needed. The remaining departments followed in rapid succession (see Figure 2). With the

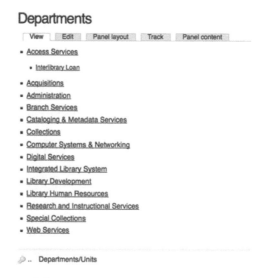

FIGURE 2 Committee and department taxonomies were created to help with organization.

basic layout similar from one department to the next, library staff reported that the ease in usability had increased significantly over the old intranet.

Not surprisingly, the task force discovered that some content did not fit neatly into departmental or committee spaces. There was no forum for informal communication within the previous intranet. Occasionally, library staff members wanted to share information about a call for proposals, to seek out a roommate for an upcoming conference, or simply to announce something fun and slightly less professional. The UH Libraries administered several e-mail lists but nothing that provided for unofficial communication within the organization. Therefore, additional pages were added to the new intranet, and anything tagged with the taxonomies would display as a feed on those pages. "Fun Outside the Stacks" was created for people to communicate about anything fun, interesting, and non-professional. Another section, "Professional Development Opportunities," was established for library staff to share announcements and opportunities for presenting, publishing, or attending workshops and conferences (see Figure 3). Incidentally, the aforementioned library e-mail lists, deemed obsolete and redundant, were eliminated with the implementation of the new intranet.

It bears mentioning that the new Drupal-based intranet overlapped with the old intranet for the first six months of 2009. During that time, no changes were permitted on the old site. Keeping the older content available during this time greatly eased the transition for library staff. The overlap also allowed time for departments and committees to reorganize and plan the information architecture of their new space, create navigational menus, and determine the focus of their pages. Planning and coordination was essential to avoid the ad hoc manner in which the old intranet pages had developed.

With the migration underway, training became paramount. Since about 130 library staff members were invested in the outcome, much attention was focused on the communication and training aspects of the project. Using a "train-the-trainer" approach, four library staff members were recruited as intranet trainers. Assigned to teach in teams of two, the intranet trainers

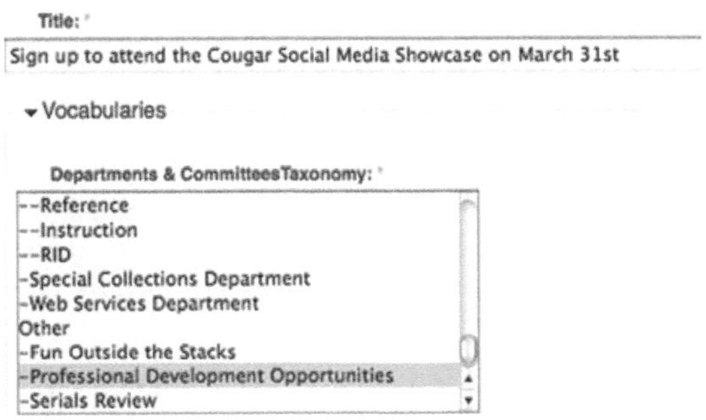

FIGURE 3 Additional taxonomies were needed to support unique content types.

offered 24 highly interactive training sessions on using the new Drupal-based site. With basic, intermediate, and advanced intranet training sessions to choose from, participants were given the flexibility to attend sessions appropriate to their skill level. The hands-on sessions were conducted in small groups, making it comfortable for library staff to ask questions and play with the new tools in a safe environment. In addition, step-by-step directions in the form of handouts were provided as a takeaway, illustrating some of the more complicated tasks within Drupal. In all, 88 library employees attended Drupal training.

CONCLUSION

While the implementation of this project was not perfect, the intranet team enjoyed many successes. Chief among these was building consensus across a variety of constituencies. The combination of a representational task force and focused discovery methods for defining the finished product helped the organization achieve its overall goals. Without buy-in, library staff members would have been hesitant to embrace such a radical change in institutional communications. Considering the breadth and diversity of library staff members was crucial. A new tool is only impressive if it works for the users and makes their jobs easier and if end users understand and appreciate what it can do for them. The training sessions held both during and since implementation of the new intranet site have been helpful in addressing this issue.

Since Drupal was chosen as the CMS in the project's planning stages, the earliness of the selection could have had a direct impact upon the project timeline and the learning curve of library staff members. Had time constraints not been an issue, it might have been prudent to explore other choices tailored to the experience and expertise of the staff members who would use it on a day-to-day basis. While this brings into question the importance of core competencies for library staff, benchmarking technology skills is not necessarily in the purview of project management or this article. While the choice of Drupal has not been judged as a hindrance in this redesign project, other organizations may want to weigh these options for themselves. To assert that things would have been better or worse in choosing an alternate CMS is merely speculation.

Maintaining a structured and accelerated schedule was another key to success, as it kept task force members focused. It prevented the project from lapsing into a vegetative state. Progress was documented and charted throughout, which kept things moving forward. There simply was no time to develop project lethargy.

The new intranet site can be considered a success in its own right (see Figure 4). Many internal communications problems, including the inability to find important material, have been solved. There are fewer places to look

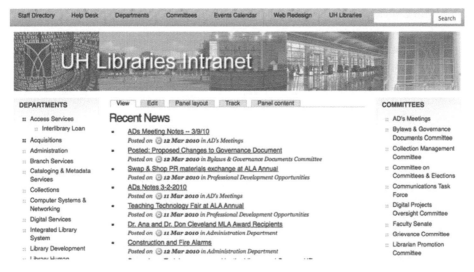

FIGURE 4 The new Drupal-based intranet has been extremely successful in bringing the UH Libraries' internal content into one place and in improving library-wide communication.

for information, and people have become more aware of internal library events and services. The library staff knows the most current information is available on the intranet. Content is shared throughout the library without a barrage of e-mail notices or additional clutter on the libraries' homepage. The redesigned intranet has the potential to enhance the library as a workplace, thereby strengthening the organization overall.

REFERENCES

Fichter, Darlene. 2001. The intranet of your dreams and nightmares. *Online* 25(5): 74–76.

———. 2006. Intranet applications for tagging and folksonomies. *Online* 30(3): 43–45.

German, Lisa. 2009. No one plans to fail, they fail to plan: The importance of structured project planning. *Technicalities* 29(3): 1, 7–9.

Kennedy, Mary Lee, and Jane Dysart, eds. 2007. *Intranets for info pros.* Medford, NJ: Information Today.

Wamsley, Lori H. 2009. Controlling project chaos: Project management for library staff. *PNLA Quarterly* 73(2): 5–6, 27.

White, Martin. 2007. Wanted: Intranet leadership. *EContent* 30(4): 30.

APPENDIX A: INTRANET SURVEY QUESTIONS

(1) How often do you go to the UH Libraries intranet?
  • Multiple times a day

- Once a day
- A few times a week
- Once a week
- Few times a month
- Never

(2) Why do you currently go to the Intranet? Please check all that apply:
- To go to a department or unit's page
- To go to a committee page
- To find statistics
- To find training materials
- To find Human Resources information
- To see what's currently going on in the library
- To read meeting minutes
- To find forms
- To find travel information
- To find links on the UH main site
- To edit a page for my supervisor
- I don't use the Intranet

(3) How useful might you find the following capabilities, if they were to be included on the intranet site? (Use a scale of very useful, somewhat useful, indifferent, not very useful, definitely not useful, I don't know what this is.)
- Upcoming Webcasts and training opportunities
- Committee meeting minutes
- Events calendar
- The ability to subscribe to all library internal news
- Knowing who is on what committee
- Polls
- Synchronous chat
- Knowing what events are going on in the Rockwell Pavilion
- Tagging
- Social bookmarking
- Printer friendly pages
- Ability to share bookmarks
- Automatically generated list of library science focused materials new in the UH Libraries
- List of technology tools available for internal use
- Sharing of patron comments
- Discussion of patron interactions
- Ability to add comments on any page on intranet
- A testing section where new tools are announced and tested by library staff
- Sharing book reviews
- Other (please specify)

Designing and Building a Collaborative Library Intranet for All

JASON J. BATTLES

Web Services Department, University of Alabama Libraries, The University of Alabama, Tuscaloosa, Alabama, USA

Intranets should provide quick and easy access to organizational information. The University of Alabama Libraries' intranet was only partially satisfying this basic expectation. Librarians could use it to find forms, policies, committee assignments, and meeting minutes, but navigating the libraries' intranet was neither quick nor easy, and it was only one of multiple sources for essential internal information. The Web Services Department of the University of Alabama Libraries was responsible for directing the redesign of the intranet. Moving to the open-source Drupal content management system (http://drupal.org), Web Services launched a revamped public Web site in January 2009. The intranet was slated for a similar redesign and conversion to Drupal by the end of the same year. The goal was to build a site that served as a center for information for library faculty and staff, provided a stream of information to keep librarians throughout the system connected, contained personalized features based on an individual's group memberships, and created a collaborative environment for all library personnel. The new intranet is a one-stop source for internal information and includes features to promote communication, professional development, and collegiality. The database-driven Drupal framework provided greater flexibility in organizing and presenting information and allowed inclusion of additional data sources. By wrapping together existing disparate information sources, adding new functionality, and giving users a platform for adding content, the new intranet is designed to be an integral part of librarians' daily workflow.

Intranets serve a basic function as storehouses of organizational information. In the case of the University of Alabama Libraries, the intranet has historically consisted of little more than forms, policies, and committee minutes. Is that enough? Some researchers recognize the potential of intranets as conduits of information that help "management and group members obtain a clearer picture of what is really going on" throughout an organization (Denton 2006, 6). Aligning the approach of this project with this broader concept of the intranet as a way to move information, the University Libraries undertook a redesign that expanded functionality by centralizing all important internal information, facilitating and promoting broad participation, and leveraging existing technologies to make the intranet easy to use and manage. The new intranet ties library faculty and staff to the daily activities and events of the organization and all of its parts while inviting them to be active contributors.

Serving the research needs of faculty and more than 28,000 students, the University Libraries are a vital part of Alabama's oldest public university. The University Libraries employ more than 120 faculty and staff in 5 libraries across campus. Within the University of Alabama Libraries, the Web Services Department is responsible for developing and maintaining Web interfaces, applications, and services for faculty and students as well as library personnel. The department consists of two library faculty and two professional staff. While directing the libraries' Web presence, the Web Services Department works diligently to include all applicable stakeholders in their projects. This consultation occurs formally in the form of the libraries' Public Interface Working Group. This group consists of library faculty and staff from units, departments, and libraries throughout the organization and provides counsel to the head of the Web Services Department, who serves as the group's chair. During the intranet redesign, Web Services frequently briefed the Public Interface Working Group and periodically updated all library personnel on the status of development. Web Services also made certain that all library faculty and staff had an opportunity to offer feedback prior to launch.

BACKGROUND

Libraries have taken a variety of approaches to intranet design, from infrastructure and functionality to content and presentation. Using a third-party application versus in-house development is one of those differences. Some librarians have had great success in building their own intranet (Engard and Park 2006). Others have relied on proven commercial and open source solutions. As it pertains to functionality, the University Libraries are moving from a narrow focus of the intranet as an information repository to an approach that enables and emphasizes collaboration among library personnel. Facilitating library faculty and staff interaction opens the potential of the intranet to serve as a decision-making and strategic tool (Denton 2006). With this in mind, the Web Services Department sought to "deliver the goods" by building a site that gave library personnel a "compelling reason to use the intranet" (Fichter 2006, 52).

DESIGN DECISIONS

The decision to use a content management system (CMS) for the new University Libraries' intranet was made in early 2008 when the Web Services Department was developing a plan for redesigning the libraries' public Web site. At that time, both the public Web site and intranet consisted almost entirely of static Web pages. Web Services researched several infrastructure options for the redesign. Flexibility in design, ease of site management, and the ability to precisely control access were all important. The department quickly recognized the capacity of CMSs to address all these needs, with the greatest advantage of CMSs being their separation of the site's data from the presentation layer. This infrastructure change would make future aesthetic site redesigns much easier, since changes to style elements would not have an impact on the database housing library content. The CMSs considered also enabled better control over access to particular content areas. This alleviated the reliance on UNIX file permissions or .htaccess directory restrictions on the server. Overall, CMSs were a much more efficient mechanism for managing the Web sites for this library.

In deciding which CMS to use, functionality, the size of the user base, and security were considered. To assist in the selection process, a Web site called "The CMS Matrix" (http://www.cmsmatrix.org) was used, which compares the attributes of more than 100 open-source and commercial CMSs. Several were reviewed, with the focus on Drupal, Joomla, and Microsoft's SharePoint. Drupal and Joomla are open source solutions. As an organization that relies on Microsoft's Exchange and Active Directory, SharePoint was also a viable candidate. However, Drupal was chosen because of its powerful access-control settings, large user community, easily modify themes for presentation, and capability to create custom modules.

The deliberation over the infrastructure of the University Libraries' redesigned public Web site and intranet and the selection of Drupal were important steps. However, as with any CMS, knowledge and expertise to configure and implement Drupal had to be gained to meet the goals for the Web environment. Proceeding with the redesign of the public Web site first may seem counterintuitive when learning a new piece of software, but the need to deliver an improved user experience and a manageable administrative environment for the public Web site was much more immediate and had an impact upon thousands of users. By the time the Drupal-based University Libraries' public Web site launched in January 2009, Web Services had learned much about how to adapt this particular CMS to the needs of this project. This knowledge provided a great head start in the work to redesign the libraries' intranet.

Having resolved the infrastructure decisions for the new intranet, the Web Services Department outlined and addressed key goals for the redesign. The desire was for the new intranet to centralize as much information as possible. The existing intranet of forms, committee minutes, and statistics was a destination that library personnel visited as needed rather than daily. The intranet omitted key pockets of information that were contained in wikis, blogs, and network drives. Understanding the organizational culture provides insight as to why this disparate information existed. All University Libraries' faculty and staff are involved in multiple groups with intranet presences. From their organizational position in units or departments to numerous faculty and staff committees, working groups, and task forces, library personnel are never tied to fewer than two of these entities. Many groups have some type of intranet content. Bringing the information for an individual's affiliations into a central location without them having to check multiple sites or pages was a primary goal. Also desired was the addition of new functionality that encouraged participation, fostered collaboration, and promoted collegiality among librarians from across the organization.

A ONE-STOP SHOP

The goal of providing an intranet that centralized all important internal information was not just about putting everything in one place but also about serving this information to users in an easily accessible and personalized way. The most significant part of the redesign that helped accomplish this goal was the incorporation of existing internal wikis into the CMS by using the third-party Organic Groups module for Drupal (http://drupal.org/project/og). Over the course of the last few years, numerous wikis were created for a variety of committees, departments, task forces, etc. Using the open source MediaWiki (http://www.mediawiki.org) software, Web Services installed and maintained these wikis. In almost every case, usage dramatically declined after a few months. Some of the wikis that remained active did so only because Web Services updated them.

The wikis fell into disuse for a few reasons. First, each wiki had a unique set of usernames and passwords. Since this information did not coincide with any existing user authentication system, wiki members quickly forgot how to log in. Initially, this led to requests for password resets, but eventually many

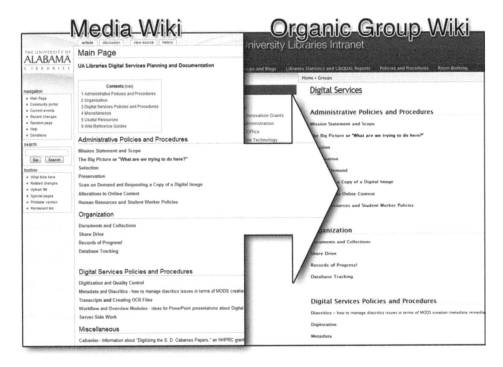

FIGURE 1 Migrating MediaWiki pages to Drupal using Organic Groups.

users stopped trying to log in. Although one of the strengths of wikis is their ease of use, they introduce yet one more markup style for users to learn (Notess 2006). Most library personnel at the University of Alabama found wiki syntax frustrating when trying to format their content.

Organic Groups (see Figure 1) enabled us to preserve the collaborative aspects of wikis while resolving the specific problems that impeded wiki usage in the environment. This module allowed the creation of both access control and content divisions based on any parameters chosen. This permitted the re-creation of wiki content and easily set wiki content editors in the Organic Group environment. With this change, library personnel could make posts unique to the groups to which they belonged. Groups can be viewable to the public or viewable only to users who are members of the group, and each individual post in a group can be public or private as well. Posts to the groups can also function as a "wiki post," allowing all members of the group to edit the post, or as normal posts, where only the creator and administrators can edit. Automatic versioning of each edit meant that, as with wikis, users could easily revert to a previous version in case of error. Group posts are edited using the CKEditor (http://drupal.org/project/ckeditor), which library faculty and staff also use for creating and editing content on the public Web site. This editor accepts plain text and uses familiar word processing application icons for formatting. Creating or updating wiki posts does not require users to make the usual selections of pathname, alias, revision, etc. that regular Drupal page or node creation entails. The Pathauto module (http://drupal.org/project/pathauto) makes it possible to set the pathname and alias.

The ability to replicate, but simplify, the wiki environment within Drupal was the largest, but not the only, usage of Organic Groups in the libraries' intranet. As mentioned, the existing intranet had content pages for committees, working groups, task forces, and a smattering of units and departments. These existed as both static and dynamic pages, but access was restricted to the head or chair of the organizational entity. Moving this content into the Organic Groups environment opened access to all members of the respective group but still enabled the traditional administrators of that content control over an individual's level of access.

With wikis and group pages in the CMS, Web Services sought to further encourage the organizational movement of information by serving up each individual's group information in a personalized feed directly to the front page of their intranet view. Using the power of the third-party Drupal Views module (http://drupal.org/project/views), users get a custom "My Groups" tab on the intranet front page (see Figure 2). This tab contains all the latest posts made to any of the groups to which they belong. Library faculty and staff no longer have to go to different sites or pages to stay current with all the information pertinent to their memberships.

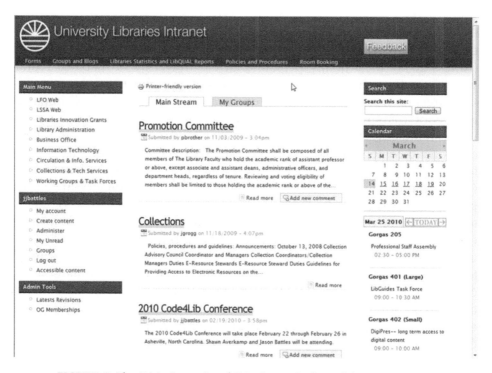

FIGURE 2 The "Main Stream" and "My Groups" tabs and the new intranet.

NEW FEATURES

Room-booking assignments for key venues within the libraries were added to the intranet's front page. The University Libraries have long relied on the open source MRBS room-booking software (http://mrbs.sourceforge.net/) for scheduling space for meetings, events, etc. During intranet development, other solutions were sought that would fit better within the CMS, but, in the end, MRBS functioned well in this environment, and its use of a MySQL database made it easy to pull into a custom Drupal module written by Web Services staff. As implemented, the right-hand column of the intranet top page includes the current day's bookings for select meeting space. This serves as much to inform library faculty and staff of what is taking place as to alert individuals of meetings they may have overlooked in their personal calendar. The custom-built MRBS module allows users to page forward a day at a time.

Included alongside the room bookings listing is Drupal's Calendar module. All users are allowed to add items to the calendar. The purpose of the calendar is to display conferences, Webinars, and other events of organizational and professional interest. The idea is that librarians from various areas throughout the University Libraries will have a shared knowledge of their colleagues' professional events. As modern librarianship is very diverse, colleagues may not be aware of the distinctiveness of specialized areas of librarianship. Systems librarians, for example, attend very different events from catalogers or serials librarians. A simple calendar does not lead to an instant understanding of those unfamiliar areas, but it does expose the entirety of the library faculty and staff to the existence of those events, and it may lead the curious to gain a better understanding of their colleagues' work.

Three other new features were added to improve communication and build collegiality among library faculty and staff. The core panel of the Web site is the "Main Stream," a chronological list of the latest page updates and additions. While the "My Groups" tab personalizes updates for the user, the "Main Stream" section gives library faculty and staff a broader view of what is going on throughout the organization. Also, a professional development section was included so users could post information on conference presentations, published articles, or reports from conferences attended. Previously, this information was disseminated only within the users' respective departments or units—or not at all. Again, this gives the entire organization information about the professional activities of their colleagues. Web Services also included a more casual "water cooler" section to the site. The intent of this area was to allow people to post about topics not necessarily related to work. For example, perhaps someone is interested in quilting or gardening and wants to find like-minded colleagues. Granted, there is no direct professional gain from such a forum, but it does build connections that translate into a richer work atmosphere.

While moving forward from the launch of the intranet, additional features will hopefully be included. The most significant addition considered is integrated chat. There are several different ways chat can be added to Drupal, including chat modules. Third-party applications like Meebo (http://www.meebo.com) can also be incorporated. Hosted chat applications, such as the open source Jabber server, are also an option. Tying chat into the Drupal profile system means online/offline status could easily be provided for users. Chat can be a useful internal tool for communication, as it is an easy way to ask a quick question with little disruption compared to a phone call or in-person visit, and it can be quicker to compose or reply to than e-mail.

AN INTRANET FOR ALL

Bringing all of the internal information important to library faculty and staff into a single Web space was key to building a highly effective intranet. Making sure all library employees could easily access, contribute, and collaborate within the intranet from anywhere was also vital to success. The University of Alabama Libraries' previous intranet relied upon unique accounts for out-of-library or off-campus access. Likewise, Web Services faculty and staff were the only library personnel able to upload files. Page editing was available to fewer than ten faculty and staff via the client-based Adobe Contribute software (http://www.adobe.com/products/contribute/). Any Web updates submitted via Contribute were reviewed by Web Services prior to publication, which could delay information getting to users. A better solution to both problems was needed.

Since intranets contain organizational information that may not always be fit for public consumption, some authentication method is usually used to validate users. For the University of Alabama Libraries' previous intranet, this method was .htaccess usernames and passwords. This method of directory access control is available via the Apache Web server (http://www.apache.org). The .htaccess usernames were not always the same as those used by the libraries' Active Directory or the campus LDAP. These differences led to frequent requests from library personnel for password changes or general inquires about how to log in to the intranet. This frustrated users and decreased use of the intranet. In the last year, IP ranges were added to the Apache configuration so that in-library faculty and staff workstations were automatically allowed into the intranet without a login. IP restriction was possible because the University of Alabama Libraries use a fixed range of IP addresses for library employee workstations that does not share network subnet addresses with public workstations. While this did help viewing access from within the libraries, off-campus and editing access still required the user to log in.

The intranet redesign sought to address this limitation by relying upon existing authentication systems. Drupal's LDAP integration module (http://drupal.org/project/ldap_integration) allowed the use of an outside authentication source for intranet logins. Since the intranet was internal to the University Libraries, Active Directory was a more appropriate source than the campus LDAP directory against which to authenticate. This meant intranet users could use their existing daily workstation login credentials to edit and upload files to the intranet from wherever they were. This simple change greatly improved intranet accessibility while also saving IT staff time in addressing username/password issues.

Having improved intranet access via Drupal's use of our existing Active Directory, the next barrier for faculty and staff usage was the ease of editing and uploading files. Coupled with a need to make intranet content editing easier was the desire to expand higher-level access to more library personnel. Historically, intranet editing privileges did not differ greatly from the public Web site. Prior to the public Web site's move into Drupal in January 2009, updates were also made via Adobe Contribute. Web Services was then responsible for reviewing and publishing the public Web site changes. The University Libraries' intranet worked the same way. Using a per-seat licensed product like Contribute limited those with access to make Web updates on both the intranet and the former public Web site. Even for those with the ability to make changes to the intranet, the publication of those changes was not instant.

The redesigned intranet's CMS made possible the inclusion of a built-in WYSIWYG editor and eliminated reliance on Contribute. This change was an essential part of opening the intranet to broader participation from library faculty and staff. The redesigned University Libraries' intranet uses the CKEditor module for Drupal (see Figure 3). This provides a Web-based, graphical editor similar to popular word-processing applications. No software is installed on any workstation. The editor has a familiar feel. The advanced user still has the ability to edit HTML code and add style elements, but the novice can avoid those complications. Even with the easy-to-use editor, the Web Services Department conducted multiple sessions with library faculty and staff to instruct them on its use. These sessions provided an opportunity to provide both assistance in usage and also explain overall changes to the editing and approval process.

One of the many goals of the redesigned intranet was expanding access and building a collaborative space for library personnel. Intranets are different from public Web sites. With public sites, there is a level of oversight needed to control editing privileges and ensure content is reviewed prior to publication. The intranet, however, is designed for the organization. Minor errors made on the intranet will get noticed by a handful of people, but errors on the public site are noticed by thousands. That is not to make light of the importance of always providing good information whether the consumer

Title: *

Digital Services 2009-2010

Body:

3. Develop monitoring systems (md5 checksum cron scripts to identify changes). [completed 20 July 2009]

4. Set up policies and procedures for access, use, and maintenance (proposed policies developed on wiki and shared, seeking feedback.)

7. **Promote UA Libraries and contribute to the profession [4] (done)**

1. Serve on the Society of American Archivists Metadata and Digital Object Round Table: participate in all meetings and perform at least one outside task in support of the agenda (missed meeting at SAA due to travel priorities and funding issues; assisted in selection of forum presentations)

2. Serve on the NISO Identifier Committee Sub-committee on Institutional Repositories: participate in all meetings and perform at least one outside task in support of the agenda [completed: analyzed and compiled survey results, July 2009; also proposed and compiled conclusions, assisting in document preparation for publication] That subcommittee has completed its work and I've been asked to serve on the NISO Identifier committee now. I accepted.

3. Seek out opportunities for publication and presentations: Submit at least 3 proposals [done: presented at CONTENTdm SE User Group Meeting; submitting book chapter in "Digitization in the Real World: Lessons Learned from Small to Medium-Sized Digitization Projects" by the Metropolitan New York Library Council; and have been accepted to present at Computers in Libraries conference in April, as well as a joint presentation with Tom and Tonio at the Coalition for Networked Information Task Force Meeting in April as well.]

4. Seek out digitization grant opportunities which will enable us to leverage the EBSCO funds to better effect, and promote the visibility of UA Libraries: submit at least one proposal (Since the NHPRC grant has been approved, we determined that this goal should be postponed. However, if Dana Chandler indicates interest, I will pursue this. I did contact representatives at the University of West Alabama to feel out possibilities for collaborative digitization, as they had expressed interest over newspapers; but have had no response.)

FIGURE 3 The WYSIWYG CKEditor.

is the public, campus, or staff; it is a balance between restraining intranet participation to protect content and encouraging participation with the risk of errors. Moving to a truly collaborative intranet means conceding some control. In the redesigned intranet, most edits are automatically published. However, there are technological solutions to make it easier to overcome the resulting problems. For example, Drupal was enabled to save each revision of a page, allowing the roll back to previous versions should a problem occur. As mentioned earlier, this feature is also one reason all of the intranet wikis were moved into Drupal.

IMPLEMENTATION PLAN

Putting the new features within the Drupal framework allowed a move forward with the implementation plan that would lead to the intranet's launch. While additional research and development time was spent mastering the modules necessary for this effort (Table 1), the bulk of the work to build the framework and move the content took place within a three-month period. In parallel with the Web Services Department's development work, all library faculty and staff responsible for the existing intranet content were contacted and a review of the policies, committee information, forms, and any other

TABLE 1 Intranet Functionality and Corresponding Third-Party Drupal Modules

Function	Modules	Description
Access	Access Control List Content Access **LDAP Integration** Login Destination **Override Node Options** **Secure Pages**	The LDAP Integration module allows login from Active Directory of another LDAP source. Secure Pages allows the use of SSL. Override Node Options enables non-admin users to promote content to the front page.
Blogs, wikis, and committees	Automatic Nodetitles **Organic Groups** Pathauto Talk **Views**	One of the unique approaches to the Drupal intranet is that former stand-alone blogs and wikis have been incorporated into Drupal while preserving their traditional functionality. Organic Groups is the linchpin of this organizational structure, with Views providing the user interface framework.
Calendar	Calendar Date	These modules make the events calendar work.
Content moderation	Module Grants Revisioning	While Organic Group posts for blogs, wikies, and committees do not go through moderation, normal pages do.
Customized content types	Content Creation Kit (CCK)	CCK allows the use of custom content types, giving added flexibility in creating pages.
Editing	CKEditor WYSIWYG Filter	The CKEditor was released the end of 2009 and includes numerous editing options through a user-friendly graphical interface.
File Management	IMCE	IMCE is used predominantly for file uploading but also provides a browse and delete capability for uploaded content.
Printer friendly pages	Printer, e-mail, and PDF versions	Printing policies, meeting minutes, and other intranet content is highly requested.
Statistics	Google Analytics	Google Analytics is widely used throughout this organization. This module allows integration with Drupal.

Note: Only the modules in bold are included in the Description section. They are the only ones described due to importance and space considerations.

information they managed was requested. In most cases, these contributors were department, unit, committee, or organizational heads. It was asked whether their intranet content could be moved into the new intranet as-is, needed updating first, or should be deleted. As Sarah Robbins, Debra Engel, and James Bierman (2006) said, "Low contribution and lack of ownership can lead to dated and inaccurate information" (262). Giving ample time for content review and updating meant the content that was moved onto the new site was current and therefore useful to library faculty and staff. Coupled with the new content being brought into the intranet, this further improved the overall quality of the end product. By launch, 20 percent of the old intranet's content was marked obsolete and deleted, and 30 percent was updated by the content providers and moved into Drupal by Web Services. The remaining 50 percent of the content was moved as-is. However, two months after launch, roughly one-quarter of that content had been updated in Drupal by the content providers themselves.

By combining the content review with the intranet framework development, a beta phase could be more quickly moved into, where feedback, usability testing, and instruction sessions for library faculty and staff could begin. During the beta phase, the existing intranet remained accessible. This gave users time to try out the redesign without being forced to switch before becoming more comfortable with the changes. A similar approach was used with the public Web site launch but with a much longer beta period because the audience was much larger and more diverse. For the intranet, feedback was collected informally through e-mail and phone calls. A feedback link was also included on the site that stored user comments in a Web-accessible MySQL database. After launch, laptops with webcams and TechSmith's Morae (http://www.techsmith.com/morae.asp) software were used to conduct one-on-one usability tests to get a more detailed look at usage of the new site. Morae is a commercial usability software application that allows one to set tasks, track mouse movement and clicks, record video, create custom surveys, and compose it all into presentations and reports. Morae was used extensively for usability tests for the public Web site redesign. Since the new intranet was designed to not only allow but promote usage by all library faculty and staff, the Web Services Department conducted multiple sessions to instruct library personnel on how to use Drupal's CKEditor implementation and walked them through posting comments, uploading files, and creating pages. The beta phase lasted several weeks before we officially switching to the new Drupal-based intranet.

A few months after launch, the effect of the redesign began to be seen. The initial move of content from the old intranet into Drupal was completed by Web Services. Once the intranet launched and library employees began receiving training on using the new framework, they took responsibility for contributing and updating intranet content. This was new ground for many library faculty and staff. Prior to the move, the intranet averaged less than five page updates a month. In the new Drupal-based intranet, there were more than 50 updates a month. The previous intranet was open to editing by fewer than ten library faculty members. Now, all library employees have the ability to add content to the intranet. Currently, almost 50 staff members have taken advantage of this capability. More than one-third of those have created content or updated pages in the last 30 days. The new intranet includes functionality previously fragmented across various wikis, blogs, and Web sites or not editable by most University Libraries' employees. Not only has the new content led to more people using the intranet, but by opening permissions to allow broad participation those pages are being visited, updated and new content have been added at a considerable rate compared to the old site.

CONCLUSION

More feedback and usability information on the redesign are still being gathered, but an initial review has shown a significant change in intranet usage. Web Services will continue to assess the work thus far, making adjustments to better meet the needs of library faculty and staff. As updates to existing applications and new technologies emerge, constant re-evaluation of how the intranet functions and whether this approach remains the best solution for users is expected. For libraries using Drupal, 2010 is expected to bring the release of Drupal 7. The Drupal 7 core will integrate some of the most used third-party modules and include significant improvements to file and image handling. Will the changes in the new release result in extensive work for those libraries using earlier Drupal versions? Is there another CMS on the horizon that will better fill the needs of this library?

There are far too many unanswered questions to know the future effect of specific products, but it is safe to say that libraries undertaking intranet redesigns have much to consider. For now, the new University Libraries' intranet fulfills the initial goals. The robust and feature-rich redesign was produced by using a specific piece of software, but there is a need to stress that this approach was not determined by the technology. Drupal obviously was an important part, but it remains merely the vehicle that allowed for the achievement of goals. The new intranet marks a dramatic leap forward for the University Libraries, not only by putting so much information at users' fingertips but also by giving them new opportunities to participate and collaborate with colleagues.

REFERENCES

Denton, Keith. 2006. Strategic intranets: The next big thing? *Corporate Communications: An International Journal* 11(1): 5–12.

Engard, Nicole C., and RayAna M. Park. 2006. Intranet 2.0: Fostering collaboration. *Online* 30(3): 16–23.

Fichter, Darlene. 2006. Making your intranet live up to its potential. *Online* 30(1): 51–53.

Notess, Greg R. 2006. Diverging Web markup choices. *Online* 30(6): 43–45.

Robbins, Sarah, Debra Engel, and James Bierman. 2006. Using the library intranet to manage Web content. *Library Hi Tech* 24(2): 261–272.

Corralling Web 2.0: Building an Intranet That Enables Individuals

AMANDA ETCHES-JOHNSON and CATHERINE BAIRD
McMaster University Library, Hamilton, Ontario, Canada

The days of top-down communication and controlled internal messages at a library organization are—or should be—behind us. Modern libraries must be fluid and flexible organizations with equally nimble internal communication infrastructures in place to keep up with the fast-paced environments that have been created in these organizations. As is the case at many institutions, McMaster University Library (about 100 employees) put a great deal of effort into public-facing resources and content, while the library intranet languished as an afterthought. Static Web pages were haphazardly created and linked to from the site's index page. As the site grew, the lack of global navigation, search functionality, and clarity about content ownership led to a large, confusing collection of pages that was increasingly difficult to maintain. In 2009, a project was undertaken to redesign the staff intranet and implement Drupal, an open-source content management system, to power the new site. This case study outlines the issues faced with the former intranet, requirements gathering, staff feedback, and usability tests performed to inform the redesign, site architecture, and Drupal modules implemented, features and benefits of the redesigned intranet, the use of the new intranet to corral existing Web 2.0/social media channels, governance, evaluation, and lessons learned from the project. Future phases of the project will focus on integrating other internal communication tools used by staff in their day-to-day work, including internal file-sharing drives, staff e-mail and instant messaging platforms, meeting scheduling software, and external document sharing tools such as Google Docs.

Consider this scenario: Michelle, a liaison librarian at a large academic library, completes a successful shift on the reference desk, during which she assisted two faculty members with finding research materials using the library's highly functional and recently redesigned Web site and catalog. During her shift, Michelle used the library's first-year experience wiki and new instructional videos on the library's YouTube channel to orient first-year students to library services and resources. Finally, she assisted a graduate teaching assistant with setting up a wiki on the library's wiki server for her second-year multimedia class.

Satisfied with her success on the reference desk, Michelle retreats to her office to work on a library committee. Searching for the committee page, she fruitlessly clicks around the library intranet, only to be frustrated by confusing navigation and repeated dead ends. Turning to the library blog directory, she finds the committee blog, where she becomes trapped in a loop that bounces her to the committee wiki, back to the intranet, then right back to the blog. Deciding not to allow her frustration to thwart her, she decides to edit the committee's page on the intranet to include links to all important online spaces and documents. When she remembers she needs to complete an online request form to have the IT department make the changes she requires, she decides to set the task aside and move on to other priorities that can be completed with fewer hurdles and roadblocks.

In *Intranets for Info Pros*, Mary Lee Kennedy states, "In highly dynamic, flattening, and porous organizations, many information professionals are struggling with what information to manage, how much effort to focus on internal or external information sharing, and when to integrate information into natural workflows" (2007, 5). This statement perfectly sums up Michelle's plight in the above scenario. While Michelle is an entirely fictional character, her experience mirrors what many staff members faced at McMaster University Library prior to its intranet redesign. As is the case at many institutions, at McMaster University Library, a great deal of effort was put into public-facing resources and content, such as the library Web site, the catalog, and various Web 2.0 channels, while the library intranet languished as an afterthought. Through three reorganizations in a two-year period, the intranet remained a dispersed collection of rarely updated, static HTML pages that did little to mirror the evolving organizational structure. And with content updates being relegated to a few individuals in the library's IT department, every aspect of the intranet needed to be rethought, from the back end to governance and ongoing maintenance.

FROM WHENCE WE CAME: THE OLD INTRANET

The former intranet, referred to internally as Libstaff, got its inauspicious start a number of years ago when library staff realized they needed an online space to record internal communications such as procedures, forms, and contact information. Static Web pages were haphazardly created and linked to from the site's index page. As the site grew, the lack of global navigation, search functionality, and clarity around content ownership led to a large, confusing collection of pages that was increasingly difficult to maintain. The extent of organization on the intranet's index page was an alphabetical list of links to content that was loosely grouped by library department. Knowledge of HTML and access to the server to publish pages were technical barriers in keeping content up to date. One common workaround strategy that developed was for library staff to create documents in a number of file formats (PDF, .doc, .xls, etc.) and have them uploaded to the intranet instead of creating well-indexed Web pages to house that content. This led to a jarring navigation experience, where clicking on a link in a navigation area would suddenly open a PDF file instead of leading to another Web page, as one might expect. Compounding this problem was a lack of standardization of file types.

In addition to site organization, the former intranet had security issues. Access was controlled by restricting IP ranges, which meant anyone with a campus IP was able to view pages on the intranet. As a result, sensitive information such as passwords and staff contact information could not be stored on the intranet. Furthermore, if a library staff member was working off-campus, use of a Virtual Private Network client was required in order to view intranet pages.

FROM THEN TO NOW: CONCEIVING THE NEW INTRANET

The system-wide frustration with the old intranet allowed quick and easy development of a list of basic requirements for the new site. These requirements included global navigation, site search, site authentication using existing staff log-in credentials, customizable permissions with different levels of access rights, simplification of content creation and maintenance, dynamic content, and a flexible underlying architecture that would allow the site to grow and evolve as the organization changed.

It was also acknowledged early on that one of the redesign's most important aspects was staff engagement and involvement in the process. This would play a role in the level of staff buy-in for the new site when it came time to launch. In response to this issue, an in-house, Web-based survey was performed prior to starting the redesign to find out more about library staff's use of and experience with the existing intranet. The following five questions were posed:

- Why do you visit the Libstaff Web site?
- What do you like about the current Libstaff Web site?
- What don't you like about the current Libstaff Web site?
- What features would you like to see on a redesigned Libstaff?
- Do you have any other comments you would like to share about Libstaff?

The survey, which was completed by 20 percent of staff, indicated:

- Staff visited the site for information on various library committees (minutes, meetings), for human resources needs (time sheets, performance documentation), to fill out forms (statistics recording, problem reporting), for policy/procedure information and help materials (staff FAQ, help sheets), and for news and current events.
- Staff liked to have one place to look for information and access to quick links.
- Some staff said they did not like anything about the site.
- Staff did not like the disorganization of the current site, the difficulty in editing and keeping it up to date, the site's general user unfriendliness and the absence of a search function, the lack of security, and the inability to easily access the site from off-campus.
- On a newly designed site, staff wanted the above items addressed, shared document drives incorporated into the site, and fun and interactive features such as photos, feeds, and comments added.

To further the level of staff engagement, about halfway through the redesign, the new intranet was presented at two all-staff forum events while it was still under construction. The intranet redesign was one of eight library projects showcased at the events and provided staff with an informal opportunity to comment on the proposed changes.

PLUMBING CONSIDERATIONS: BUILDING THE BACK END

It was realized early on that a database-driven content management system (CMS) would be the only option to fulfill many of the desired technical requirements, which included authentication, good indexing for site search, and author permissions. Fortunately, the authors had prior experience working with Drupal (http://drupal.org), an open source CMS, as part of a library Web site redesign just a few months earlier. The valuable experience gained from customizing Drupal for the library Web site redesign meant it instantly

TABLE 1 Mapping Requirements to Drupal Functionality

Requirements	Drupal functionality
Global navigation	Drupal Themes allowed this to be accomplished easily
Site search	All content is housed in a database ("nodes") and indexed, allowing for excellent content indexing and search
Site authentication using existing staff logins	Decided on using Drupal's built-in authentication
Customizable permissions with different levels of access rights	User management within Drupal core allows for granular access and editing permissions
Simplification of content creation and maintenance	Content templates coupled with user permissions streamlines the creation and editing of content
Dynamic content	Drupal's database-driven back end allows the display of content in different ways and places on the site and easy inclusion of content from other channels using RSS syndication
Flexible underlying architecture	Drupal's database back end is extensible; also the core Taxonomy module allows for standardized architecture across the site

became the number-one choice for the intranet implementation. Armed with the requirements list and valuable staff feedback, requirements were mapped with Drupal's core functionality and added modules (see Table 1).

One of Drupal's biggest selling points is that the core application can suitably serve any Web site, and with the addition of user-developed modules that plug into the framework, just about any additional functionality that was needed could easily be added. Table 2 provides a list of modules implemented on the intranet and what each module accomplished.

INFORMATION ARCHITECTURE AND NAVIGATION

Kim Guenther (2003) and Allison J. Head (2000) both noted that one of the major pitfalls of intranet design is organizing sites around a library's organizational structure. Being sensitive to this, the project began by creating a content inventory of the old intranet, allowing the effective categorization of that content. After some contemplation over how the site was likely to grow, the following "types" of content were decided on: department, service, project, committee, staff training and development, and policy and procedure. Working with the taxonomy and Content Creation Kit (CCK) modules in Drupal, content types and templates were created for each type. With these content types, discrete items such as a department could be easily added, deleted, or moved to reflect organizational changes. Furthermore, having "committee" and "project" content types allowed a link to be made

TABLE 2 Drupal Modules Implemented

Drupal module	Features/output
Content Creation Kit (CCK)	Allows site administrators to create templates for different types of content; e.g., committee template contains the following fields: committee name, chair/lead, links (optional), mandate, membership, start/end date, minutes (optional), additional information (optional)
Comment	Allows logged-in users to comment on any page or node
Contact	Provides contact forms for every user on the site, allowing staff to contact each other easily
Development	For site administrators, allows for easy troubleshooting
FCKEditor	WYSIWYG editor that allows site authors to format content using recognizable formatting icons (no knowledge of HTML required to add/edit site content)
Filters: Headings Anchors and Table of Contents	Provides authors with an easy way to create internal page links and tables of contents for pages based on headings
Forum	Threaded discussion boards for improved communication and discussion among staff
Menu	Allows site administrators to easily customize and maintain global navigation
Path & Pathauto	Allows users to rename URLs and set up predetermined paths for certain types of content
Poll	Useful for getting staff feedback quickly and engaging staff in fun ways
Profile	Staff can edit their own profiles, add avatars, etc.
Search	Essential for site-wide searching
Statistics & Google Analytics	Usage statistics and analytics to help with continuously improving the site
Taxonomy	Powers the organization of the site based on category terms
Taxonomy Breadcrumb	Allows site administrators to build page breadcrumbs based on taxonomy terms in use
Upload	Allows individual site authors to upload files to pages; particularly useful for committee minutes
Views	Provides site administrators with various options for displaying the database-driven content

from committees and projects to certain departments and for those linked relationships to just as easily be changed in the event of departmental reorganization.

The global navigation, which appears across the top of all intranet pages, consisted of the six content types and a seventh label for "Old Stuff." Three different taxonomies were used on the site to assist with generating dynamic views, and all new pages must be identified as a certain content type (department, committee, service, project, etc.). Additionally, the views module in Drupal was used to dynamically update the landing pages for each of the items in the global navigation. Thus, the landing page for "Department" lists all the library departments in an alphabetical browse-all list. To move an item to "Old Stuff," it simply needs to be tagged as such. Site authors could also give this item a secondary tag, such as "committee" or "project," to indicate an old committee or completed project. Some items, such as policies and procedures, are also tagged as belonging to a certain library department.

CONSIDERING GOVERNANCE

The core ability in Drupal was used to customize site permissions and designated five different user roles with varying degrees of editing access to content. Compared to the former staff intranet, this greatly increased the number of people who were able to maintain and update certain portions of the Web site. With the new site, 48 staff members—nearly half of the staffing complement—hold one of the five editing roles (see Table 3). Permission to create new pages that were not a designated content type was not granted widely. To maintain the integrity of the site architecture, only site administrators were given the right to perform this task.

FEATURES AND BENEFITS

Peter Griffiths outlines the following useful features for intranets: collaborative working, communities of interest, discussion groups, electronic forms, internal newsletters, internal trade, search facilities, and training materials

TABLE 3 Site Governance and Permissions

Role on the intranet	Level of permission	Role in the library
Administrator	Create and edit any content type; administer all other functionality on the site (taxonomies, menus, blocks, comments); create new pages	User Experience Librarian (public website manager), Marketing, Communications and Outreach Librarian
Committee/service/ project editor	Create and edit committees, services, and projects	All staff who chair/lead a project, service, or committee
Department editor	Edit department landing page content; create and edit policies and procedures; edit any page	Department heads, designated department contacts
Staff training editor	Create and edit staff training development pages	Teaching and Learning Librarian, other staff as designated
General page editor	Edit page content	Miscellaneous staff as designated

(2000, 165–166). In redesigning this intranet, these features were kept in the forefront of the development plans and were incorporated wherever possible.

Real-time content creation, allowing for easy collaboration on the fly, is easily accommodated by the new intranet. Mandatory standardized fields for new intranet pages, such as new projects or new committees, bring consistency to these staple categories of content. Small-scale ventures, such as a small weeding project, can just as easily be represented on the intranet as large-scale initiatives, such as the creation of a new integrated library system. Previously, information about smaller projects may not have been captured except on local hard drives and through e-mail exchanges among certain staff. As a result, there may have been little to no access to this information by other library staff. Now, those working on smaller projects can easily document their work on a single intranet page. Conversely, large-scale initiatives that use a project wiki for day-to-day workflow and documentation are often dense with information. Staff members who may not be involved with the project but require some basic piece of information about the project are able to avoid sifting through an entire wiki and access key project information from the intranet's project page, from which a link to the project wiki is provided.

Drupal's poll module has provided some much needed fun and informality to the site. An initial poll was used to gauge the reaction to the new site, asking staff to vote on how much they liked or disliked the new design and organization, the results of which indicated the initial reaction was overwhelmingly positive. Subsequent polls allowed staff to vote on their favorite campus eatery, summer vacation activities, and new TV shows.

As indicated in Table 2, the comment module in Drupal was implemented to allow staff members to post comments on any page. Allowing comments on the site has proven to be very useful, particularly after the launch of the new site. The staff use comments to request changes to pages and suggest improvements. Since site administrators are notified of new comments, the ability exists to respond to comments quickly and make iterative changes on the site. More recently, staff members have been observed addressing problems themselves by responding to each other using comments rather than waiting for a response from site administrators.

Finally, one of the single biggest feature enhancements to the intranet is the addition of search functionality. Whereas on the previous staff intranet library, staff were forced to browse and stumble through page after page to find the information they were looking for, the new site has a search box on every page. Usability testing has proven that many staff members use the search function when looking for information, some choosing to use it exclusively over browsing. As usability best practices have taught, it is crucial to provide users with multiple avenues to access the information they are seeking, and the addition of a search box on all pages fulfills that principle on the new intranet.

CORRALLING WEB 2.0 CHANNELS

Two years prior to the intranet redesign, McMaster University Library staff took part in a very successful Learning 2.0/23 Things (http://macetg.blog.lib.mcmaster.ca/about-learning-20-mac/) staff program. The success of the program, coupled with the launch of internally hosted blog and wiki software (the highly dysfunctional intranet at the time), led staff to enthusiastically create blogs and wikis to organize projects and committees and handle internal communication within service areas (and effectively circumvent the existing intranet). These tools have satisfied their purposes very well, and while the goal of the intranet redesign was not to replace them, the intention was to use the new site as a single jumping-off point for all internal library communication.

In practical terms, this means that all library departments, committees, and projects have at least a single page on the new intranet, with links to all other relevant documentation. For example, a library committee has a committee page on the new intranet and is listed with all other existing committees. If the committee uses a blog or wiki to record meeting minutes or share documentation, then the committee intranet page simply links to that space. This structure allows committee chairs to continue using blogs and wikis for communication/documentation purposes, but it also enables library staff members, who might not be familiar with a particular committee, to easily access all committee information in a central location.

In addition to bringing together the blog and wiki channels already in use, the library intranet also needed to provide access to the staff newsletter, which was converted to a blog at the same time as the intranet redesign. Drupal's aggregator module was used to syndicate an RSS feed of the staff newsletter blog posts and display the most recent headlines on the main page, making the intranet the number-one referring site to the staff newsletter blog. This crucial connection fulfills two important requirements: providing dynamic content on the intranet's homepage and connecting the staff newsletter to the intranet, which allows staff to easily discover new newsletter posts instead of forcing them to bookmark the newsletter site and visit the site for updates.

To further satisfy the dynamic content requirement, a slideshow of recent images added to the library's Flickr account was included on the intranet homepage. As one of many social media channels in use at the library, the redesigned intranet was once again chosen as a hub for our social media activities rather than to supplant those activities. In addition to providing the homepage with some much needed visual interest, the image stream also allows library staff members to easily view images of recent library events and staff celebrations rather than forcing them to visit our Flickr page to view this content, as was the case prior to the redesign.

THE BIG REVEAL: ROLL OUT, TRAINING, AND POST-LAUNCH EVALUATION

As with any major project, success often hinges on good communication. In an effort to keep staff informed about the redesign throughout the project, existing communication channels, such as e-mail and all-staff meetings, were used to remind staff of the project at regular intervals. A few weeks prior to the official launch, staff were invited to participate in one of six hour-long training sessions that were designed to familiarize them with the new Web site prior to flipping the switch on the new intranet and removing access to the old one.

The training sessions were customized to the groups in attendance. For example, those staff who were likely to only view the new site and not be involved with behind-the-scenes changes and updates were given training on logging in, changing log-in passwords, a general orientation to the new site, and basic information about editing permissions on the new Web site so they would know the procedure for requesting a change or update. Other groups of staff who would be involved with editing and updating were also trained on attaching files, creating new content, and adding and deleting related links. Step-by-step documentation of the training was recorded in a wiki, including annotated screenshots and written instructions, so staff would be able to refer back to directions on how to perform various tasks.

A few months after the initial launch, a second Web-based staff survey was conducted, modeled closely on the first survey about the previous intranet. The following questions were asked:

- Why do you visit the Libstaff Web site?
- What do you like about the Libstaff Web site?
- What don't you like about the Libstaff Web site?
- What other features would you like to see on Libstaff?
- Do you have any other comments you would like to share about Libstaff?

The same response rate as the first survey was maintained, with 20 percent of staff responding. Results included the following insights:

- Staff continue to visit the site for information on committees and projects, human resources needs, to fill out forms, and for policies and procedures and library news.

- Staff reported liking the site's ease of use, new design, easy home access, security, access to the staff newsletter, and good content and new items such as polls, comments, photos, and a search function.
- Staff did not like that they still had problems finding information, although, in contrast to the last survey, no one said the site lacked organization. Some did not like the new layout, the labels, or the multiple navigation areas; some did not like the default font size and colors.
- One outstanding feature staff requested but was not rolled into the redesign was access to documents on shared staff drives, a feature currently under investigation for phase two of the redesign.

In response to lingering findability issues, a round of usability testing was conducted. Eight staff members from departments across the library were observed while they attempted to complete nine tasks on the redesigned site. Findings from the usability testing include some accessibility and design issues and some confusion over labels in use in global navigation. While changes are made to the site based on feedback and test results, it is planned that a 90-day cycle of conducting usability tests and making iterative changes be maintained.

CONTEMPLATING THE TAKEAWAYS: LESSONS LEARNED FROM THE REDESIGN

As any good project management text will say, it is crucial to plan the transition from project to maintenance. In this case, it was learned that the intranet cannot simply be redesigned as a discrete project and then left to sort itself out. Even with distributed editing, the intranet needs central ownership to realize complete adoption by individuals in the organization and become an invaluable tool. Since Drupal allows for distributed editing and content management, the project coordinators naively underestimated the amount of post-launch governance necessary for the new staff intranet.

Staff feedback also indicated that the importance of providing a unified experience was overlooked. Redesigning an entire Web site, implementing a CMS, and revising all content is a large project with a broad mandate. In this single-minded effort to improve the intranet, there was a failure to scope out other tools that affect library staff's ability to carry out their day-to-day tasks, including internal file sharing drives, communication tools (e-mail, IM), meeting scheduling software, and external document sharing tools (like Google Docs). Plans for phase two of the redesign include these tools within scope to provide a more unified experience for library staff.

Finally, despite everything that is known about the importance of resisting the urge to design an intranet around an organization's structure, there was a frequent temptation to turn to the institution's organizational chart to inform navigation and labeling decisions. Ongoing user testing and feedback from staff helps the project's coordinators to resist this temptation, but it serves as a repeated lesson on a daily basis.

CONCLUSION

While phase two of the intranet redesign project aims to target some of the outstanding issues described, staff feedback and testing have already proven that the new site is a vast improvement. Content is more findable, thanks to good indexing, site search, and consistent navigation; staff workflows have been streamlined as a result of easier site access and simplified content creation and maintenance; the scalability of the site architecture ensures the intranet will grow and evolve more comfortably with the organization; and the integration of the library's existing 2.0 channels provides a more seamless experience for library staff. Thinking back to fictional librarian "Michelle" and the hurdles and roadblocks she faced with the former site, it is certain she would have a much better experience with the library's intranet today.

REFERENCES

Griffiths, Peter. 2000. Your intranet. In *Managing your internet and intranet services: The information and library professional's guide to strategy*, 161–173. London: Library Association.

Guenther, Kim. 2003. Ten steps to intranet success. *Online* 27(1): 66–69.

Head, Alison J. 2000. Demystifying intranet design. *Online* 24(4): 36–42.

Kennedy, Mary Lee. 2007. Introduction. In *Intranets for info pros*, ed. Mary Lee Kennedy and Jane Dysart, 1–13. Medford, NJ: Information Today.

Index

Page numbers in *Italics* represent tables.
Page numbers in **Bold** represent figures.